As Time Goes By

BY KITTY FREUND.
1ST JULY 2019

Published by Kitty Freund 2019

Copyright©Kitty Freund 2019

All rights reserved. No part of this publication may be reproduced, stored in a retrieval system, or transmitted, in any form or by any means, electronic, mechanical, photocopy, recording or otherwise without the prior permission of the copyright owner.

ISBN 978-1-5272-4718-5

Printed by Dolman Scott Ltd
www.dolmanscott.co.uk

Dedication:

*To my son and daughter: David and Erica,
my three grandchildren: Louisa, Esther, Leah
and my dear friends.*

INTRODUCTION:

Having reached the age of 107 years, I describe some of the many events in my life in England and in South Africa.

ACKNOWLEDGEMENTS:

Being partially sighted and no longer able to see to read or write, I dictated my life history to kind friends. Lynda Spiro was a regular visitor helping me with the script. My daughter Erica did the major work of editing and bringing this book to fruition. She accompanied me for two years to a writer's class tutored by Helen Harris. My son David helped, and when the course at the London Jewish Cultural Centre came to an end, we joined with members of our class and met regularly to develop our scripts.

Special thanks to Dr Cavendish and Dr Suppree, at the Hodford Road Surgery, for keeping me in good health. To Dr Vrappi, in the Cardiology Dept at the Royal Free Hospital who never failed to give me and my old heart the best of attention.

A special thanks to my home helps, who have assisted me so much over the years.

At the North Western Reform Synagogue, in Alyth Gardens, I am described as 'the mother of the Synagogue.' I appreciate the attention the rabbis and the congregation bestow on me, particularly Rabbi Goldsmith. I want to thank Rabbi Danny Rich, who provided comfort and support for our family at a time of need.

I treasure the memory of fellow members of the Leo Baeck Lodge, with whom I spent many happy hours. The names of these my dear friends are too numerous to mention.

Thank you to the AJR (Association of Jewish Refugees), who over the years have supported in countless ways my husband and myself. They introduced me to Amina Brightwell, who visits me regularly.

My grandchildren have enriched my life and I enjoy my old age and thank all the people that have helped me write my Memoir.

MY FAVOURITE QUOATATIONS:

My favourite quotations:

You must remember this, a kiss is still a kiss, a sigh is still a sigh
The fundamental things apply, as time goes by.

My favourite quote:
'As Time Goes By', written by Dooley Wilson for the film *Casablanca*

Be good sweet maid and let who will be clever
Do noble deeds not dream them, all day long:

Aunt Esther's favourite quote:
Poem *Youth Farewell*, by Charles Kingsley

There is a tide in the affairs of men
Which taken at its flood leads onto fortune
Omitted all the days of their life
Is bound in shallows and in miseries

Hans's favourite quote:
Julius Caesar, by William Shakespeare.

Page viii: Picture of Kitty, aged 21 years

CONTENTS

Chapters

1. Childhood 1
2. Leaving Liverpool 8
3. Jewish Orphanage, West Norwood, South London 11
4. Memories of Norwood and the First World War 33
5. Life with my Mother 36
6. My New School, Streatham Hill High School 44
7. School and Family Outings 51
8. My Cousin Marcus returns from the First World War 55
9. Teacher Training 58
10. Sneaking off to the Locarno Dance Hall 62
11. Moving to Westbourne Terrace. My first Teaching Post 65
12. Going to Dances. Meeting Hans 75
13. Hans Leaves for South Africa 81
14. Letters from South Africa. Sad News 88
15. I leave for South Africa. A new life begins 95
16. My Decision to Remain 108
17. Our Wedding 113
18. War is Declared. Bad News 117

19 The Official Account of Hans's Escape (Dispatches)............125

20 Our baby David is born 132

21 The War is Over! Our baby Erica is born 141

22 A Visit to the Family in London..154

23 Return to South Africa. Pollsmoor..157

24 Special Events. Bergvliet 173

25 David's Barmitzvah 177

26 Sad News in the Family 181

27 Hans visits Berlin for the first time after the War.................183

28 Growing fears about the Political Situation.......................... 186

29 Our Move to Rondebosch..189

30 Life Changes..193

31 Illness in the Family. Auntie Annie 199

32 Our new home in Golders Green 203

33 A New Life in England..208

34 Holidays and Trips 213

35 The Changes over my Life-time 218

36 Reflections. My 106th Birthday... 223

Kitty aged 21 years.

Chapter One.

CHILDHOOD

My childhood was fairly unusual. I was born on the 5th day of February 1913, at 45 Fern Grove, Sefton Park, Liverpool. I was named Ghita Pearson, but was always called Kitty. To begin, I will describe what I know about our family history.

My father was Samuel Pearson. My mother was Flora Reed. They were married on 21st June 1911, at Princes Road Synagogue, Toxteth Park, Liverpool. The marriage failed, and when I was eighteen months old my mother left my father and came to London.

I know little about my father. In 1885, his father came from Bialystock, from the Pale of Settlement in the north-eastern corner of Poland. He changed his name from Perlovich to Pearson. I understand that he was well versed in the Torah. He was obviously a good businessman and from small beginnings he founded the thriving firm of J. Pearson & Co. He had over fifty employees and they produced all types of glass-work: from glass cutting, picture framing, glass bevelling, silvering and the making of Victorian over-mantles. He lived at 9 Bentley Road, a very prestigious address, where the cotton brokers, ship owners and rich merchants lived. This area was near to the Princes Road Synagogue.

I remember visiting my paternal grandparents, the Pearsons, on only one occasion. When I was about to start my secondary education, my mother wanted the Pearsons to contribute towards the expense of my schooling, and so she took me to visit my grandparents. I remember standing next to my mother, who was seated in an upright chair, and my grandmother and grandfather Pearson sat opposite in easy chairs. I noted that Mrs Pearson was crying, and that surprised me. They were prepared to help financially, but said they wanted to see more of me. However, I was fortunate enough to win a London County Council scholarship, which provided for my needs, and so my mother did not take up their offer.

My mother's family, on the other hand, struggled. My grandfather Jacob Reed came to England from Eivenitz, a very small village in Polish Russia, near Minsk. His name was originally Jacob Beyer Voynoff. He was born at Eivenitz, Poland, within the Empire of Russia, on 19th March 1848. He was the son of Louis and Frieda Voynoff. On arrival in Hull, the Customs official handed him a document to complete, but he could not read English. 'Can't you read?' said the official, and so Jacob, in bewilderment, repeated back: 'Read?', and consequently the Customs officer put down his name as 'Reed'. He travelled across to Liverpool en route to America, but probably ran out of money, so he remained in Liverpool.

I have always been told that his father was one of the bandmasters to the Tsar's army and, despite the limitations for Jews living in St. Petersburg, he was able to reside there.

He married Kitty Schock, who was not yet twenty-one, on 19th May 1870 at Seel Street Synagogue. Kitty Schock was born in 1849 and her name was Ghita, known as Kate or Kitty. Her mother and father, my great grandparents, were Heyman (1828) and Rebecca Schock. These are the few facts about my great-grandmother: For Orthodox Jewish women when they married, they are required to shave off their hair and wear a sheitle (wig). I was told that when my grandmother arrived in England, she took off her sheitle and threw it into the fire. I know that she had a relation, probably her brother, who sold sponges in the streets of Liverpool and lived until he was one hundred, which was remarkable in those days. Heyman was one of three brothers, all of whom had large families.

One of my grandmother's brothers was dressed as a girl so that he could avoid being conscripted into the Tsar's army.

My grandmother, after whom I am named, was a teacher at the Liverpool Hebrew School. On her marriage certificate she signed her name, but my grandfather was unable to write English and so made a mark. Jacob worked for established tailors, taking on 'piece work', making up garments. Most of the garments were completed successfully, but occasionally they were returned to be modified. Within a few years, he opened up his own tailoring shop in Bold Street, Liverpool, where he made and designed ladies' costumes and dresses. It was the fashion in those times to wear costumes, and he employed several tailoring workers.

Kitty's first baby miscarried, but then on 4th July 1873, she gave birth to another child they named Esther. Later, in 1889, when the baby Annie was born, her mother contracted puerperal fever and at the age of thirty-eight she died, leaving the eldest Esther (b. 1873), aged fourteen, Clara (1879), followed by Louisa (1882), my mother Flora (1884), aged four, Louis (1886), aged two, and the newly born baby Annie (1889). This was before the days of penicillin, and three mothers were similarly infected and tragically died. Kitty's mother and father (Nachman) took little Louis into their care, and the baby Annie was handed over to a wet nurse. They tried to get my mother Flora admitted to the Jewish Orphanage, but this request was refused, probably because she was too young.

When the eldest sister, Esther, visited the wet nurse and saw baby Annie, she was shocked at her condition. The baby's hair was full of nits. Esther, then aged fourteen, immediately took the baby away from the wet nurse and decided she would look after her, together with the other children, Louisa, Clara and Flora. They then fed the baby with a bottle. Little Annie contracted rickets due to an unbalanced diet. Kitty's father and mother, the Schocks, came frequently to the home, and Auntie Esther used to quote them: 'Esther vu bist do in parlour or in kitchen?'

Jacob, my grandfather suffered from asthma. When he was too ill to work, one of his daughters would have to get help from a welfare board called the *Tontine* to get money to buy food and clothes. I believe this was a charity run by the Liverpool Synagogue. The Welfare State did not exist in those days, and life was a struggle. Their father made all the children's clothes from the left-over material from his tailoring work. These bits of material are called cabbage.

Despite being so poor and without a mother, I remember asking my Aunt Esther, then aged 100, the question: 'When were you the happiest?' She thought a moment and then replied, 'When our family were all together.'

The Liverpool Hebrew School was an important part of their everyday lives – all the children went to the school, now called the 'King David'. Over time, Esther, Louisa and Annie became pupil-teachers. In this way they had further education after the age of fourteen.

The children were all devoted to their father Jacob, who they loved dearly and called 'Dadda'. As he grew older and became frail, each one took it in turn to care for him. I think he must have been a very loveable person. I have a letter written by Auntie Esther's husband Myer after Jacob had visited them. It was shortly after she had married and had left the family home. Myer writes how much they enjoyed his company and how he hoped he would visit often. Myer made it clear to his father-in-law how happy he was, describing his marriage to Esther as 'married bliss'. Jacob died in January 1913, at the age of sixty-five, a week before I was born.

The family followed the Orthodox Jewish way of life and kept all the traditional laws of Judaism. The Shul in Hope Place was quite close to the school, and this was the centre of the Jewish community in Liverpool.

The family shared a love of clothes and fashion. Much later in my life, when I was living in Pretoria, South Africa, I met a Mrs Halford at a party and she announced to everyone that the Reeds were the best-dressed family in Liverpool. (Mrs Halford came out to South Africa from Liverpool to live in Uppington, a remote 'dorp' in the Transvaal, and travelled over bush-land for many miles by ox wagon.)

The Reeds were extremely fond of hats, which everyone wore in those days. On one of my visits to England, after I had moved to live in South Africa, my Aunt Esther asked me to help her dispose of all her hats. She had a little story to tell about each one. She held each hat most lovingly in her hand and related something of their history. I am told that my mother had a hat that was so large that she had to take it off to enter a railway carriage.

The family were quite articulate and were never afraid to express their opinions quite freely. They were talented in different ways. Esther and Clara were members of a Dramatic Society. Esther had a gift for reciting poetry, and it was hearing her recite a poem that, it is said, led Myer, her future husband, to fall in love with her. My Aunt Esther, who cared for me, often recited the lines from a poem: 'How are you, my handsome and noble child?'. I did not take this as a personal compliment and knew she was quoting something. Or when she saw that my room was untidy, she would not reproach me, but would say: ''Tis not every maid that keeps her room so neat.'

My Aunt Clara, with her bright red, golden hair, was probably the most arresting of the sisters. After she married, she had a family of four boys, which kept her very busy, although at some stage she opened a jewellery shop in Bold Street.

My Aunt Louisa won a Queen's Scholarship to Liverpool University, where she gained a first-class degree in English, which in those days was an unusual achievement for a woman. She loved music and had a library of books on poetry and music. Sadly, she became very depressed, stopped eating and finally drowned herself in the Mersey.

My mother was deeply upset at such a sad loss and it affected the whole family. My mother had the least education of any of the family, leaving school at fourteen. She was very practical, and she told me she missed out a lot at school as her teacher asked her to look after her baby, who was in a pram outside the classroom. She did this instead of attending lessons. I was never aware of her lack of education, and she endeared herself greatly to my daughter Erica by her special ability to invent endless stories centred around a girl called 'Bertha', who always did something naughty and ended up being told off. I wonder if this was based on her own memory of her childhood, though I remember my Aunt Esther saying how their father never had to tell them off as they were all very good children.

Of all the sisters, my mother Flora, had the greatest flair for choosing clothes and could buy dresses for all of us, which would fit us and look beautiful. She had a very good eye for fashion and an acute visual sense.

Louis was extremely talented both in music and in art. He won a scholarship to study the violin and as a boy could recognise any piece of classical music and give you details. He won a scholarship to the Liverpool School of Architecture.

Chapter One. Childhood

As a student, he designed the Prayer House for the Jewish Cemetery and the entrance doors to the Liverpool Philharmonic Concert Hall, home of the Liverpool Orchestra. Both are still in use and have been designated heritage status. All his life he painted, and I still have a beautiful painting of his father that he did at the age of eighteen. Following a life-time living in Northern Ireland, selling his paintings and holding exhibitions, after his death he was described as the 'Picasso of Northern Ireland'. He also learnt his father's trade. He could design and cut clothes, and after his father died he took over the business.

Annie, the baby of the family, was from the earliest stage a gifted pianist and musician. I was told that from the age of four she played the piano for her class. Because of her talent, she had one or two lessons, paid for by one of the richer members of the community, but mostly taught herself to read music. She was musically very gifted and could play the piano beautifully, having an exceptional talent to play by ear, and could improvise an accompaniment in whatever key was needed. She played the piano for the silent film cinemas and went on to play the organ at Norwood and, much later, to play the organ in the synagogue in South Africa.

Chapter Two.
LEAVING LIVERPOOL

My mother married Samuel Pearson at the Princes Road Synagogue, but the marriage was a failure. My mother discovered that her husband was mean with money. She also found that he had a fierce temper. This was a very difficult time for her – her beloved Dada had died the week before I was born, and her elder sister Esther and Myer had moved to London. My mother decided to leave her husband and take me as a young baby with her. In those days, this was a very exceptional thing to do. At first, she went back to stay with Annie at her father's rented house. She was unable to get a divorce. This was a very difficult transaction in those days and only possible for rich people.

She did obtain what was called a legal separation, which meant that she was allowed to live apart from her husband. In addition, he was supposed to support her by paying her thirty shillings a week, a satisfactory sum in those days. He refused to do this and, rather than pay her anything and probably because he wanted to avoid the war, he emigrated to Boston, USA. He lived there for the rest of his life. What a difficult situation to be in. It meant my mother could never re-marry. It was not possible to be divorced until after A. P. Herbert's Divorce Act (1937).

Samuel, by going to America, had cut himself off from his family, as he had been the eldest son of a thriving family business. I believe

Chapter Two. Leaving Liverpool

he opened a shop in Boston selling antique furniture. I know little else about him, except that he was a skilled poker worker. This is the art of burning a design with a heated metal point into wood or leather. He made such things as card boxes sculptured out with a hot poker, and the objects were painted. For years I had one of these boxes. In the early years, I believe he used to write to me, but still have a watch that he sent to me which had inscribed on the back 'To Kitty from her father'. I knew about the letters, but my mother never gave them to me, so I never saw them and never replied.

My mother was therefore in a very difficult position and did not know where to turn. In desperation, she came to London. At the time, I was eighteen months old. She took me to her elder sister Esther and asked her to look after me while she looked for work. My Aunt and her husband Myer had, three years earlier, become headmaster and matron of the Jews Hospital and Orphan Asylum, as it was then called. It was later renamed the Jewish Orphanage, situated in West Norwood, South London. This was a highly prestigious and responsible appointment. They also had the care of their son Frank, who was physically handicapped and could only walk with crutches.

Nevertheless, they agreed to look after me. Esther, after her mother died, had taken responsibility of her brothers and sisters, and here she was continuing this role. Esther asked Marcus, her eldest son, if he would agree to their taking me in, and he was in favour of this. She also had to ask permission from the Norwood Committee to allow me to stay. She then hired a nurse-maid to look after me and so, at the age of eighteen months, I was installed as part of my Aunt Esther's family in the orphanage.

My mother found work at an officers' convalescent home in Park Lane, but later found employment as the manager in charge of a block of flats for working women. It was called the Ladies Residential Chambers in Chenies Street, off Tottenham Court Road. In those days, it was unusual for women from a certain social stratum to be away from home and work, and this building provided respectable living quarters. The residents had a flat but no cooking facilities, and were expected to eat from time to time in the dining room. Each time, they paid for the meal. My mother was responsible for the entire organisation, which included being in charge of the porter, the kitchen staff, ordering the food and everything entailed in the running of this unique accommodation for ladies. Many well-known suffragettes were residents and also frequent visitors.

Considering that my mother had no qualifications, it was much to her credit and personality that she obtained this post, which she kept for many years. In spite of the suffragette ethos that women should be allowed to work, they did not allow me to stay with my mother on a permanent basis. Nevertheless, as I grew older, I stayed with her fairly frequently. She visited me every Sunday and usually one other day during the week. We also went on holidays together.

Chapter Three.

JEWISH ORPHANAGE, WEST NORWOOD, SOUTH LONDON

I recall various members of the family describing how I was as a baby.

My mother told me that the doctor said: 'This baby has been on earth before.' This was said because I seemed very alert and as soon as I was born had my eyes wide open and was looking about me. My mother told me about the difficulties she encountered when she decided to leave my father. It was not something often done in those days. My mother brought me to London when I was eighteen months old. She left me with her elder sister Esther and her husband Myer, who were then the Headmaster and Matron of the Norwood Jewish Hospital and Orphan Asylum.

My mother went out to look for work. I believe that I was frequently sucking a dummy. One evening, my uncle, in disgust, threw the dummy out of the window, but I screamed so hard that he was forced to go outside and in the dark search with a torch to find it. So, I think, they must have had their hands full looking after me. When I was ten or twelve years old, I often heard from old Norwood boys and girls, when they came back to visit, 'I remember seeing you being bathed when you were a baby.' This embarrassed me greatly at the time.

From the age of eighteen months till nineteen years old, I lived in Norwood Orphanage with my Aunt Esther and her family. I took much for granted and perhaps did not appreciate many of their virtues. People change over the years. I changed, and they changed, but I will try to remember how we were in those early years at Norwood.

My aunt and uncle, with their two sons, came to Norwood in 1910. I am told that they were promised a house of their own which would be built for them in the grounds. It is clear that they wanted a life apart from the full-time employment at the institution, but the events of the First World War prevented that promise from ever being carried out. Marcus was twelve years old and Frank nine. This meant that they had to adapt themselves as best they could and find a degree of private family life wherever possible. For this reason, we had breakfast and lunches together in the lower sitting room. This room was also used as a part-time office for my Aunt Esther. At the weekend, we joined the staff for meals.

Upstairs, my bedroom had a door leading to Daddy Myer and Aunt Esther's bedroom. As previously mentioned, my Aunt Esther took responsibility for the care of the family after the death of her mother. That was when she was only fourteen years old. She married Myer Kaizer when she was twenty-four in 1896. He was then a teacher at the Liverpool Hebrew School. When Myer Kaizer was appointed as Headmaster of the South London Jewish School, Borough Road, they moved to London. Here, their son Marcus was born. Marcus always boasted he was a true cockney, because he was born within the sound of Bow bells.

When Aunt Esther gave birth to her second son, Frank, difficulties with the delivery arose and mistakes were made. The baby was

Chapter Three. Jewish Orphanage, West Norwood, South London

delivered by forceps and in the process the spinal cord was damaged. He had no strength in his legs and he walked by pulling himself along with two sticks. Frank's history might have been different had he been born today. Whenever anyone mentioned his birth, it caused my aunt great distress. It was probably there at the back of her mind, throughout her life, the worry about this son, Frank. This year, when my daughter Erica was doing some research into Frank's history, I found out that Aunt Esther had lost a third baby called William, who had only lived for twenty-four hours.

In spite of this, she was of a cheerful disposition and my memory of her was that she was quite prepared to sing, recite and make humorous comments about whatever was happening at the time. She always looked well dressed, took trouble with her hair and on occasions could look very elegant, probably with my mother's influence and encouragement. My mother was the one who always took the lead in the clothes that the family wore. Auntie Esther enjoyed reading and would usually send one of the older girls to the Boots Library (all Boots chemists had a library in those days). She did not join the Public Library. I do not know why.

Auntie Esther enjoyed knitting and knitted all the socks for the family. The family also enjoyed playing cards.

I never heard Myer and Esther exchange a cross word, with one exception: when the three sisters and Daddy Myer played bridge. After each game, the family held intense inquests to discover what had gone right or gone wrong. Because of this, Marcus and I never ever wanted to learn the game.

'What will you do in your old age?' the family said to us in amazement. Maybe they had a point there. Although Esther did not play any sport, she always followed a routine of physical exercises, throughout her long life.

When I came to live with them, my Aunt employed a children's nurse to look after me. The first nursemaid was called Eva Cheeseman, and later it was our well-loved Nellie Ling. As well as caring for me, she served the meals, did the family washing and mending. We called Nellie '*Motlow*' after a song: '*Nellie my own true loved one. Wait till the clouds roll by.*' Nellie was always busy and frequently, when asked to do too much, was heard to remark to my Aunt: 'Mrs Kaye, I have only one pair of hands.'

I had my breakfast downstairs with Daddy Myer, my two cousins Marcus and Frank. Although he was my uncle by marriage, from the first I called him Daddy Myer because, for me, he was my father. But his wife, who was my Aunt, I called Auntie Esther. I think they enjoyed having a little girl.

Children were in those days encouraged to believe in fairies and Daddy Myer enjoyed making up fairy names for the whole family. My fairy name was *Mashloona Inkadom* and Frank's name was *Cigano Cigaretsky* (Frank was a big smoker). I was, I believe, a little, round, fat child, and my cousin Marcus called me *Globula*, so that I called him *Gobbie* in return. Gobbie he remained always.

I remember sometimes when I had done something considered 'naughty', Daddy Myer would say: 'We will have to have the little girl over the way instead of you.' I do not remember feeling insecure, but I remember looking over the lawn, across the railway line to the road on the other side to see if I could see this little girl loitering around, ready to take my place, but I never could see her.

I have other glimpses of memory. The first was when I was standing in the maid's dining room, which was off the large kitchen at the rear of the Big Dining Hall. Each domestic member of staff had their own seat at the table and I was often given my lunch there; but, on this occasion, I looked at the cook's chair that had been decorated

Chapter Three. Jewish Orphanage, West Norwood, South London

with flowers and I knew then that our cook, who was called Toy, had died. I remember thinking: I am two and a half years old and this is a very important occasion.

My Aunt Esther was responsible for the entire domestic staff who worked in the orphanage. She had a pleasing, friendly and encouraging manner with everyone. Older girls, when they returned to Norwood on a visit, would say to me: 'I was her favourite', which says a lot about how she appeared to them as they grew older.

The Gabriel Home

When I was old enough, I went to the Gabriel Home, where I was put in the 'babies class'. The Gabriel Home had recently been built in 1910 by Mrs Jane Gabriel. It was built to accommodate younger children between the ages of five and seven. I loved being in this class. There was a big sand-tray, a doll's house, as well as many sense training toys. This must have been quite advanced for those days, and following the influence of Friedrich Froebel, a German educationalist, famous for laying the foundations for modern education. These ideas, very new at this time, recognised the special and unique needs of child development.

We sat on little round chairs that we were able to lift up ourselves, and small wooden tables suitable for two children. The teacher at that time was Miss Brodie, the younger sister of Rabbi Brodie, later to become the Chief Rabbi. She had just graduated from college. We learnt the first stages of reading and I recall our reader had a Beefeater on the front cover. I remember the moment when I realised that I could read. We had to learn the Hebrew sounds from a rather boring book. We loved listening to stories as well as responding to music. When Miss Brodie left to go to Australia – my dear Aunt Annie took her place.

In the babies class, I made two special friends called Annie Bernstein and Rosie Rosen, and we remained friends right through the school and afterwards. Annie Bernstein eventually went to America, but I kept this friendship with Rosie Rosen for many years. She married a Norwood old scholar.

As soon as I grew a little older, I was free to go to many parts of this large building. I could visit the kitchens, sit by the fire with the cat and dog in the maid's dining room, go down into the laundry, where they put me on a moving roller used for the ironing of sheets, or I could play with the girls in the quadrangle. I was always welcome, and people made a fuss of me.

Another incident occurred when I was four. We used to sit outside on a seat, and I would walk down the long drive to the sweet shop, which was next to the gate (every Norwood child can remember their favourite sweet from this shop). I had two pennies to buy a little bag of homemade coconut candy.

On one occasion, I met Eva Cheeseman's little sister and she must have been about ten years old. She said to me: 'Would you like to come and see my father?' Her father was a chimney-sweep, and this was something special, to see his face blackened from the soot.

She took me by the hand and we walked a little way up Knight's Hill, to one of the narrower roads where she lived. When her mother saw us, she said to her young daughter, 'Take her back immediately!' As we returned, we found my Aunt Esther and Daddy Myer and a few members of the staff looking anxiously up and down the road. I remember wondering what all the fuss was about.

The following Sunday, my mother said to me, 'If anyone says to you come with me and I will give you a bag of sweets – you must

Chapter Three. Jewish Orphanage, West Norwood, South London

never go.' I could not imagine anyone being so generous as to give me sweets.

Now I shall tell you about my home in the Jews Hospital and Orphan Asylum (later re-named the Jewish Orphanage), where I lived from the age of eighteen months until I was nineteen years old.

This institution was opposite the West Norwood railway station in South London and was approached by a long drive darkened by trees and shrubs on either side. When you reached the lodge-keeper's pretty cottage, you could see for the first time this large, imposing institution. The building was designed not unlike the famous Dulwich Public College, which you could see in the distance. The building was surrounded by eight acres of fields and playgrounds.

I remember that, as you approached the four-storey building, you could hear the sounds of four hundred and fifty children at play, which is like no other sound I know.

If it was school time, you could hear the teachers' voices booming forth. Then, if it was Shabbat, you would hear the sound of the children singing. The shape of the building, mostly built in red brick, followed the design of a capital letter E. The two ends formed large protruding bays. One end was for the boys, where there were classrooms on the ground floor with the dormitories above. Similarly, on the girls' side there were classrooms with dormitories to the second and third floors. On both sides, iron fire escapes twisted from the top to the bottom of the buildings. There were separate entrances for the girls and for the boys. Visitors approached the building through the front porch with a large wooden door.

On either side of the porch were the staff living quarters, and bedrooms on the second and third floors. More bedrooms existed under the eaves, making a fourth floor. You came first into a large entrance hall with an ornate marble staircase. At the top of the staircase, I remember an original huge oil painting which dominated the hall. It was called: *'By the Waters of Babylon, we sat down and wept when we remembered Zion'*. I do not know what happened to this painting, nor can I trace its origins at present.

On either side of this painting were two ornate doors that led to the children's dining hall, which seated all four hundred children. The room was very grand, and had a high ceiling, supported by columns. At one end was a large pipe organ and at the other end a minstrel gallery that led from the first floor to the infirmary, where children went when they were sick. A marble bust of Queen Victoria looked down over our heads and many children enjoyed taking off her crown as they went across to the infirmary. I remember how the light streamed through the large stained-glass windows that skirted along the walls and even through a glass dome roof. Large painted portraits of many of the benefactors lined the walls. The walls were tiled.

At the furthest side of the hall were the kitchen pantries and sculleries, as well as the domestic staff's dining hall.

On the first floor there were large rooms, with high ceilings, that led off long corridors on either side of the porch. Below were two quadrangles, with overhead cover so that children could play in wet weather. In addition, on the boys' side of the building there was a basement where the boys practised if they were in the brass band. Another room was used as a club for the older boys. Large boilers heated pipes that ran from the basement to many parts of the building. A stoker and an engineer, Mr Landgrave, looked after the heating system.

On the other side in the basement was the laundry, where all the washing for the whole institution was undertaken by laundry maids.

Chapter Three. Jewish Orphanage, West Norwood, South London

The first room on the ground floor, called the 'lower sitting room', was where my Aunt Esther and family had their meals. It also served as an office for my Aunt, with glass-enclosed bookshelves lining the walls from shoulder height to the picture rail. The books belonged to the Behrend Reference Library and were used by the staff. There was a large dining table in the middle, covered with an elaborate cloth. As a child, I loved to sit underneath the table and felt as if I was in a little cave of my own. In one corner of the room was a pretty piano, which I learnt to play. There was a fire-place, and a spirit stove which heated water, as there were no electric kettles in those days. When it steamed, my cousin Marcus used to say, 'We are steaming the Babylonian Talmud,' referring to the heavy books which were enclosed in the shelves above.

A telephone with a mouthpiece and separate receiver rested on top of a cabinet in the corner, and by pressing down various pegs you could contact the infirmary or the Headmaster's office and other places. I do not remember many people using a telephone in those days, although I was allowed to ring my mother. I pressed down a peg to get an outside line, then a voice would say, 'Number please', and I would reply 'Museum 2503', which was my mother's number, and I would then be able to speak to her. I remember that the Norwood number was Streatham '1676'.

Next to this sitting room was a long, imposing room for holding meetings of the House Committee. The elaborately carved oak table had two special chairs for the Chairman and President, and these were of the most ornate design. This room housed more reference books, mostly of a Jewish nature, the major part of the Behren Library. Leading off from this room was a rather grand toilet with wash basins. I have no idea what happened to the books belonging to that library when the building was sold. I know that my cousin Harold found one of its books by chance in a secondhand book shop. There was a revolving bookshelf which contained many volumes of the *Encyclopaedia Britannica*. Next to this was a gramophone on wheels with a huge horn, and it had to be wound up by hand. A further door led off into a strong-room where, I presume, wages were kept. Large tins of boiled sweets were also kept in the strong-room. In the committee room, there was a side table where a full-time secretary carried out her work for the headmaster.

On the other side of the hall was what we called the 'best sitting room'. This contained a lot of attractive, antique furniture which Daddy Myer had collected, some of which I still have in my own house. Next door was the staff dining-room, where teachers, nurses and assistant matrons had their meals. There was no room for us to eat there during the week, but at the weekend our family joined the staff.

The grounds were extensive, and on the top field was a large workshop, where a fully qualified craft teacher taught the boys woodwork and metalwork. Many of the boys became cabinet-makers when they left.

The orphanage had a very long history. There were many prestigious members on the committee. A member of the Royal Family was always a patron. In my time, Sir Anthony de Rothschild was the President. He only came to Norwood on prize-giving day, and always looked very serious during the lovely performances given by the children. When I was a little girl, I tried with my dancing to make him smile, but did not succeed.

The house committee met each month. Lady Spielman was the chairwoman, with Sir Basil Henriques as a member of this committee. When they came, the drive was full of very expensive chauffeur-driven cars, and the smell of cigars was everywhere. Our 'best' sitting room always had a large tray of whisky and soda for the gentlemen and probably tea for the ladies.

Chapter Three. Jewish Orphanage, West Norwood, South London

I would like to tell you something about the routines and the daily life in the institution. The big bell rang at half past six for the children to get up, wash, dress and make their beds. I think the younger children each had an older child, called their guardian, to help them. After a hastily recited morning prayer, the children went in for breakfast. After this, each child had a small domestic chore, according to their age and ability. It could be polishing a door knob or sweeping a room. The boys' quadrangle always smelt of boot polish. They had to polish their boots very carefully. There were three or four shamuses in the shul, and I often saw the boys taking a swig of the kosher wine. At ten to nine, school started. The girls' classes and the boys' classes were held in separate rooms.

For four days a week the lessons always started with Hebrew – that is translating and reading Hebrew, learning about the Jewish festivals and listening to stories from the Bible. Remember, there was no Israel in those days, so that Hebrew was taught as a dead language, as one would learn Latin. We learnt arithmetic, which meant much time spent on mental arithmetic. We used to recite the 'times tables' in a sort of chant. I particularly enjoyed composition – today you would call it 'creative writing'. In each class we had a poetry book and were expected to learn a poem each week.

Nearly every classroom had a piano, which was used to accompany our singing. Songs were written on the blackboard in tonic sol-fah. We did not learn by rote. I can remember many of those songs today and do still with much pleasure. I remember: *Soldier, soldier, will you marry me with your musket, fife and drum* and the song *In Dublin fair city*.

Reading was always encouraged, and each class had its own library up to Standard Five. Then children were allowed to go to the Public Library on Knight's Hill. There was a very strange procedure in use when I first started going to the library. You looked up the title of the book on two large boards and found its number. You then went to see if the number on another board was either marked in red or blue. If it was red, this meant the book was out; and if it was blue, you could go to the librarian and collect it. At some stage, they changed the routine and you could go into the library to look at the books. I was shocked and thought that every book would be stolen; but, of course, I was wrong.

Hygiene was taught throughout the school, although I never really learnt how a baby was born, something I really wanted to know. In Standards Six and Seven we had classes on Citizenship. We staged our own election and I was chosen as the Labour candidate. I was supposed to speak on Tariff Reform, but did not have a clue about it, but I spoke nevertheless. I was not voted in.

After school, especially in the summer, we had wonderful games outside. Sport was compulsory for everyone. The boys played football and cricket and the girls netball and hockey. The boys had a PE teacher. Sergeant Warren was his name. He took them for drill, consisting of different exercises, such as standing on each other's shoulders to make a pyramid. There were other seasonal games which we girls enjoyed very much, such as varieties of hopscotch, skipping, mobs and gobs (a game with little stones), spinning with tops and a very complicated game called Diablo. This consisted of two sticks and a reel of string and a kind of top.

In the winter, special programmes were arranged. At the weekends, there was always Friday night Shul. The older girls sat downstairs, opposite the boys, which was quite remarkable for those days. After the service, we had a Debating Society. Teachers and older children would give a talk, which was followed by general discussion. Boys and girls were encouraged to catch the speaker's eye so that he or she could be allowed to speak. As for me, I never had the nerve, although Daddy Myer tried to encourage me. I would look away towards the Ark, terrified that he would catch my eye and I might be called upon. I never spoke, but once, when I was a little older, I gave a talk on the story of Dreyfus, which was quite topical at the time. I remember my family discussing this case.

Shabbat morning was again Shul, the girls sitting upstairs and taking no part in the service. We looked down upon the boys and the masters, who were quite active. There were many barmitzvahs and much singing, which we enjoyed. We also listened with interest to the sermons, because the Headmaster and teachers all knew what would interest children.

I particularly remember one sermon in which Daddy Myer described the pogroms that were going on at that time in the Pale of Settlement. Funds were being collected to help the victims. He said: 'I know you are all generous children and will want to contribute.' I watched the little heads rise proudly and I thought what a good idea that, instead of always accepting charity, they felt that they had a chance to give instead to others who were needy.

After Shul, everyone went for a walk in the local neighbourhood – to Streatham Common, Brockwell Park, Crystal Palace, or Dulwich Art Gallery, which was free; or much nearer home – the recreation ground.

Daddy Myer sat outside to watch the children leaving for their walks. The boys would have to raise their caps, while brothers and sisters collected their smaller siblings from the Gabriel Home. There was a special dinner on Saturday. Never chicken, which was too expensive – always a roast of beef or mutton. On Saturday evenings in the winter, entertainment was arranged. Concert parties came, or there would be lantern slides – no films, remember. The large gramophone was wheeled into the dining room and illustrating slides accompanied the music. I remember a man singing *Many brave hearts are asleep in the deep*, and the lantern slide showed a man carefully covered in his striped bathing costume lying full length, under the sea, leaning on his elbow.

Sunday morning was Hebrew for two hours and oh, what a joy when the St. Luke's church bells rang, accompanied by our dog, who howled at the sound, which let us know it would soon be time to go out and play.

Special Events at Norwood

On Sunday afternoons once a month was 'Visiting Day', when the relations came to visit. Mothers always brought hamisha food, which was much appreciated after the plain and wholesome food given by the institution. Of course, some children did not have a visitor, because they had no family, or their relatives lived too far away. When speaking to the teachers, some children had to translate, as their parents only spoke Yiddish.

There was also one special woman whose name I have forgotten, a person who had no children in the orphanage but who would bring sweets specially for these children. I called her Darling, because she always said to them, 'Here, darling, this is for you', and these children would accept the gift rather solemnly. I think this was typical of the generosity of the people at that time.

On other Sundays, Ministers would bring members of their synagogue to visit the orphanage, as every synagogue had an orphan aid society that contributed funds to Norwood. On these occasions, there was usually a football match, umpired by Daddy Myer, who at one time could have become a professional footballer for Liverpool. The boys' brass band would play cheerful music. The children were given a little party. During the winter evenings, different programmes were arranged. Monday evening was hobby night, and you could choose which hobby you wished to pursue. For the girls, there was embroidery and crochet. There was also a Dramatic Society, and for the little ones a society called Various Occupations, which I thought was called 'Fairies Occupations'!

Boys and girls joined a choir if they wished, and every year produced one of the Gilbert and Sullivan operettas, such as *Trial by Jury* or *HMS Pinafore*, and parts of *Iolanthe* were performed. I can sing most of *Trial by Jury* to this day. Boys could also choose chess, which Daddy Myer taught. Boxing and early wireless operations were other activities. I once received a crystal set, and when you put on the earphone and wriggled the cat's whisker, music came out, which was marvellous. From Tuesday to Thursday was homework and letter-writing.

We knew what to expect each day and throughout the year and, in a way, this gave security. For example, in early January the whole school was invited to watch the pantomime at the Croydon Grand Theatre. The whole school would catch the train at West Norwood. The train was marked P, which we thought was for pantomime. We would march through Croydon and the kind owners of the theatre put the children into the dress circle and stalls. The show could be *Puss in Boots* or *Robin Hood*, but all were full of humour, songs and dancing. The part I liked best was the story. Each child received an orange and a silver shilling when they left. When the owners sold the theatre, they put in a clause that stipulated that the Norwood children should always be invited to come to the theatre.

We all looked forward to the festival of Pesach, the Jewish Passover, and the wonderful two Seders are times I remember all my life.

To see the shining faces of all the children, to hear a little child recite the four questions and to join in the singing, was unforgettable. Nothing in the world is quite like it.

The next event was the visit to the Royal Tournament at Olympia, followed by high tea provided by H. M. Lyons. The whole school enjoyed this. Next came the visit to the zoo. I remember most of all the roaring of the lions and, oh, the smell in the Lion House and the embarrassing monkeys, because of their pink bottoms. The visit to the zoo included a special tea, with watercress sandwiches followed by, wonder of wonders, ice-cream! Then came the summer holidays. Before the children could go home for the holidays, their homes were inspected, and if they were not passed, the children were not allowed to go home. Tears were shed if this happened. Many of the children lived around Brick Lane, in London's East End, where some quarters were cramped and overcrowded. To make up for their disappointment, a good summer programme was arranged for those who stayed behind.

Many boys went to the Jewish Lads Brigade Camp at Deal Church.

Some of the girls went to Seaford, where they stayed in bungalows which were formerly ex-army barracks. The bungalows were hired from the Jewish Free School.

At Norwood, we always had a sports day on the front lawn, when you could take part in the egg and spoon race, the sack race and the tug of war. One of the school masters would bellow the details of the forthcoming races through a megaphone. During the holiday, we would all go to the little cinema. Of course, they were all silent films in those days, except for a pianist, who played suitable music to accompany the films. There was usually an exciting episode that would end with the note 'to be continued in our next', and probably an early Charlie Chaplin film, too. We would also be given the chance to spend a little money, either three-pence or at the very most a sixpence. Many children would not get further than the sweet shop at the corner of the road, and whenever I meet old scholars they talk in loving terms about the coconut-candy and other kinds of

Chapter Three. Jewish Orphanage, West Norwood, South London

sweets they would buy. Some of us would walk from West Norwood as far as Tulse Hill to look in the toy shops in search of finding a toy of the best value.

In Tulse Hill, there was a particular toy shop, where the sales lady's hands trembled. If you saw something you fancied in the shop window, you forced yourself to gather up your courage and enter the shop to buy from the woman with the shaking hands.

After the summer holidays, we looked forward to Succoth more than the other High Holy days. All the children had the chance to visit our Succah, hung with fruit and sweet-smelling herbs. Every child could walk through the Succah and then be given fruit. There were also the Succoth concerts.

Every girl belonged to a club, where they played games such as Ludo and Snakes and Ladders. Each club was expected to give a concert in the Committee Room for their friends. The songs at these concerts were usually popular songs of the day. A group of girls would sing, wearing a borrowed top hat, or there would be dances and sketches.

Cakes and biscuits were on the Committee Room table, which had been pushed to the side, and club members would urge their friends to take a bite. The club member who was offering these delights would say, 'Don't be shy, take one.' Then, when the visitors had left, all the cakes were soon demolished by the club members. And so the year would pass, ending with the celebration of Channukah, the Festival of Lights. There was no mention whatsoever of Christmas, which was never celebrated.

Daddy Myer. The Principal and Headmaster

Now to tell you about my Aunt Esther's husband. His original name was Kiezar, but in Liverpool it became Kaizer, which was very unfortunate, especially during the First World War; so much so, that my cousin Marcus insisted they changed their name from Kaizer to Kaye. Myer Kaye was, strictly speaking, only a relation by marriage – but he was to all intents and purposes my father, and I called him *Daddy Myer*.

He was born in Liverpool on 26th August 1871. As far as I know, his father came from the Ukraine. I know very little about his past history, except for two points of interest: the first was that in the Ukraine his father was connected with the timber trade, and his grandfather remembered seeing Napoleon's men returning defeated from Russia.

Daddy Myer's father died when he was four years old, leaving his mother a widow, Sarah Kiezer, formerly Bluck, with four children: William Fraser, Henrietta, Sophia and Myer. Soon after this, his mother re-married to a Mr Berman, who also had six children. Two more children were born, and after some time the second husband died, leaving behind a big, destitute family. Myer always told me that he could not describe how very poor they were and what a struggle it was to survive.

In spite of this, he became a pupil-teacher at the Liverpool Hebrew School. In 1903, he attended Liverpool University and obtained a BSc degree in Science with a Division One pass. During this time, he was still teaching at Liverpool Hebrew School. He won a special prize from the Earl of Derby, as the best student of his year. He was active in football and played as half back for the University. In those days, Liverpool was still an amateur football club, but was in the process of becoming professional. He played amateur football for Liverpool and considered becoming a professional footballer, but my Aunt Esther was against this. He was a master at chess. He trained teachers in religious studies, became a school examiner, and visited the USA as an educationalist. He had an outstanding career.

His first appointment as a Headmaster was in 1896, at the Borough Road Hebrew School in South London. This school was near a market noted for its food, where many Jewish people worked. He was appointed in charge of the Bell Lane Technical School. He used to conduct the choir in the Borough Synagogue and instructed all the Jewish teachers in London in Hebrew and Religion.

The family returned to Liverpool in 1900, when he became Headmaster of his former school next to the synagogue at Hope Place. He encouraged the parents to adopt what was in those days a very progressive attitude, not to keep children confined at home studying the Torah (it was feared that if parents allowed children to venture out to play in the streets of Liverpool, they would be targets for attack), but he wished to encourage them to attend school regularly and benefit from an all-round education, play sports and from that be best fitted to participate in the life of Liverpool. He encouraged boys to learn to box, so that they could defend themselves if there was need. He started an Old Boys' Scholars' Association to help raise funds to expand the school and build new classrooms. Later, when he moved to Norwood as Headmaster, he kept in contact with the old scholars and returned for their important reunions.

In 1910, he was appointed Headmaster of the Jews Hospital and Orphan Asylum, as Norwood Orphanage was then called. He and my Aunt Esther had the overall responsibility for the running of this large institution, which later became known as Norwood The Jewish Orphanage. They were answerable to the Committee, who consisted of important members of the Jewish community. No easy task.

He represented the ultimate authority at Norwood when I was there and within our own family this was the same, and I regarded him in the same way throughout my life. He was never domineering, and although he was strict and held high expectations of others, he never boasted about himself and was eager to appreciate and praise other people's successes. He had many interests – too numerous to mention all of them. He coached the boys at football and would run vigorously around when refereeing matches. He did not use the staff tennis court, but enjoyed a good game of golf.

He bought all the family furniture – hunting for antiques both locally and in Brighton. If anything needed repairing, he would take out his carpentry tools and say: 'I am fixing fine furniture.' At a later date, he searched for first editions at secondhand book shops and built up an interesting library. He enjoyed good conversation about current affairs with friends and teachers. He was always intent on enlightening the children and widening their horizons. He read many newspapers, especially the *Jewish Chronicle* and *The News Chronicle*, which was a Liberal paper, supporting Lloyd George. In the evenings, he loved his game of cards – first solo and then bridge – or would sit of an evening solving a chess problem with his portable chess set. He was quite mechanically minded and owned a motor-bike with side-car and later a three-wheeled motor car.

He had a pleasant appearance and always looked trim and neat in his bespoke suits. When I praised what I thought was a new suit, he would open up his jacket and show me that the suit had been made ten years earlier. He had a pleasing voice, which, of course, we heard during the synagogue service. I could go on at greater length, but as you see, he truly was a most remarkable person.

Chapter Three. Jewish Orphanage, West Norwood, South London

The People in the Orphanage

I would like to tell you about some of the people at Norwood. Firstly, the children themselves. Of course, I was in close contact with the girls and got to know many of them very well; less so for the boys. The girls who became my friends were generous and supportive of each other. Each one had her own sad story, having lost a parent or even both parents. Despite this, they were warm-hearted and cared for one another.

Many children found it very difficult when they first arrived at Norwood, and one or two tried to run home. The Headmaster was always worried about this, and relieved when he heard they were safe. When the mother brought them back, he made as if he did not to want to accept them again. He wanted them to realise that they were the lucky ones who had got into the orphanage because as many as were admitted so were as many refused. Nevertheless, he did eventually take them back after a mother's plea. You only have to read some of Israel Zangwill's books to know the degree of poverty and deprivation of those times. This was before the Welfare State, and many poor and struggling families relied upon the soup kitchens provided by the Jewish community for their sustenance.

In the end, most of the children adapted themselves and settled down. I never heard a child swear, and there were no drugs or anything like that; boys probably did a bit of smoking on the quiet. Bullying among the boys was strongly discouraged. If there was a quarrel among the girls, one of the quarrellers would say, 'She thinks herself everybody.' That expression seemed to help smooth over the argument.

The teachers were all qualified and worked hard. They worked long hours teaching during the school day and then after-hours had responsibilities and more duties. Most of the men teachers were married and lived in houses close by, where they could go when off duty. There were no married woman teachers in those days. If a woman teacher married, she had to leave. Mrs Rosenthal was the Headteacher and when she married she left. There were also Assistant Matrons, who, together with two dress-makers, made and mended the girls' clothes and linen. Remember, all children wore a uniform, which was not easily washable, so the girls always wore cotton pinafores during the day for protection.

Alice worked full-time with tending to the boys' clothes. She occupied a large room on the third floor. She washed, mended, sewed on buttons and patched up tears on the boys' clothing from morning till night. I remember one occasion when a teacher asked, 'Where's Kaplan?', and the boys replied quite seriously, 'He's up in Alice.'

Besides the laundry maids and other staff, I must mention Bridget Brown and her sister Maggie, who came from Ireland and who did all the cooking. Both of them, although they were devout Catholics and attended their church regularly, knew more about Kashrut than anyone.

As well as the residential staff, there were a number of other people who came in daily, such as the doctor who came at least two or three times a week. Also, the dentist made regular visits. Both the doctor and dentist kept careful records, unusual for those days. Mr Stern, the barber from Tulse Hill, came and cut everyone's hair.

If a child felt unwell, they were given an extra mug of milk with egg to drink.

The Reed Family: Backrow: Flora (my mother), Louisa, Esther, Clara, Annie, Dada Jacob, Louis.

My mother holds me. I am 8 weeks old.

1911. Berlin. Hans as a baby with his father.

My mother Flora and my Aunt Clara.

My cousins Marcus and Frank with their mother, my Aunt Esther at the seaside.

My Aunt Esther and my cousin Marcus.

Norwood Jewish Orphanage.

I dress up as a fairy.

Here I am with Annabel, my doll.

Here I am standing beside mother.

I dress up as a Red-Cross nurse.

Chapter Four.

MEMORIES OF NORWOOD DURING THE FIRST WORLD WAR

Another time, I remember sitting, having my lunch upstairs in the bedroom, when Marcus came in and asked me if I would give him my teddy bear as a mascot. This was because he was about to go away to be an air-pilot and fight in the First World War. I remember saying 'No', and offering him a doll instead. Her name was Betty Blue, and I was not keen on her. He must have taken the teddy, though I never noticed, and when he was shot down over Germany and taken as a prisoner of war – later, a wounded teddy bear came back with his belongings. Someone had bandaged the teddy bear and I have it to this day. Incidentally, it was made in Germany and sewed together, and you can see the stitching.

West Norwood was close to the Crystal Palace. It was a landmark recognised by the German bombers as indicating that they had arrived in London. They flew low over our area. When there was an air raid, all the children came downstairs with a blanket and sat in the downstairs corridors and were given cocoa and sweets. I assume that when the bombers flew over it was kept dark, but I do not remember. I was not frightened, but thought it was very exciting. The bombing was nothing like what occurred in the Second World

War, but I remember that three big houses were destroyed near to Streatham Hill station.

My cousin Marcus joined the Royal Flying Corps after he left Dulwich College at nearly eighteen years old. Even to train as an air-pilot was dangerous. Marcus was interviewed by an archivist from the Royal Air Force Museum in Hendon, and all the details of his training as a pilot and his subsequent career in the Royal Air Force during the First and Second World Wars are recorded there. I have a copy of this information.

In the Second World War, Marcus went missing for six months.

I remember the postman coming to the front door and holding up a letter and saying, 'Give this to your Aunt.' I went upstairs straight away and gave it to Auntie Esther, who was standing in her bedroom. Her son, my cousin Marcus, had been missing for six months. This letter gave Auntie Esther wonderful news, that although he was a prisoner-of-war, he was alive. She said she would never forget that moment because, until a letter arrived to say that he was a prisoner-of-war, she had lived in dread and at least she knew then he was still alive. As soon as possible, we started sending him letters, and many teachers and children joined with our correspondence. I know that he got parcels of food from Mrs Melchior and her sister, Lady Spielman, the Chair Lady of Norwood House Committee. Mrs Melchior lived in Denmark and was able to send him bread and even eggs. He said he could not have survived without that extra food, as the rationing in Germany was meagre and food was scarce. Marcus had been wounded in the arm and it was only because of the care from two Russian doctors, who were prisoners-of-war with him, that he managed to overcome this serious wound.

The Melchior family became well known, and when the Germans were advancing on Denmark in the Second World War, her son, who was a rabbi, was the one who told the congregation of his Shul not to delay, but to flee from Denmark as quickly as possible and to go to Sweden.

We also sent Marcus food parcels. Marcus wrote back to us to thank us and said he would love some food from a certain shop that turned out to be a stationer, where you could buy maps. Daddy Myer took the hint and started sending him whatever he wanted – obviously to help him escape. It was considered the duty of every officer who was a prisoner-of-war to try to escape. One day, Daddy Myer received a letter from the War Office or the Foreign Office – I don't know which – asking him to come to see them. Daddy Myer was very worried, but when he arrived there they said, 'I believe you are trying to send your son material to help him escape. What can we do to help you?'

They sent things in tins – like wire cutters. After the war, we found out that Marcus had attempted to escape twice. First time he was disguised as a plumber – the second time he got as far as the northern border – the Customs officers were looking for smugglers, and when they spoke to Marcus, they realised that he was not German. On both occasions, he was returned to the prisoner-of-war camp and put in solitary confinement. When he finally returned to England after the war, like many other returning soldiers, he had to have treatment for depression. He finally was offered a place at **Gonville & Cauis College Cambridge**, where he took a degree in Mechanical Engineering. He won a **tripos**, which meant that he had passed with high honours in all three subjects.

Chapter Five.
LIFE WITH MY MOTHER

My mother visited me every Sunday, and she would put me to bed and would say, 'I will tuck you in like a parcel.' As I grew older, I would go to stay with her at weekends or during the holiday. My mother was now in charge of a block of flats in Chenies Street, off Tottenham Court Road. It was built especially for working women, and this was a respectable and safe place where they could live. They were expected to have some of their meals in the residence.

My mother had her own flat, but she did not have permission for me to live with her permanently. She was responsible for the management of the entire residence. In the morning, we would walk along Tottenham Court Road, past *Sherns*, a lovely fruit shop, and we'd look in the windows of Heals, the furniture shop, which is still there today, and so to *Shoolbreds*, a large general store supplying practically everything. *Shoolbreds* also sold clothes and at Christmas held special entertainment for children. I remember lovely puppet shows and my mother took me there at least twice a day to enjoy them.

On some afternoons we crossed over Tottenham Court Road and walked along Mortimer Street, until we reached a road called Wells Street. Here, my Uncle Louis (Reed), who had come from Liverpool, rented a flat. His flat consisted of two bedrooms and a sitting room.

Chapter Five. Life with my Mother

It was a basement flat – there was a nice kitchen, but no bathroom. The bath was in the kitchen, with a big board over it. The toilet was outside the flat on the landing. He had married Anne Humphreys and was working at Dickins & Jones in Regent's Street, making any alterations needed to women's costumes. Later, he became a well-established costume and coat designer, first at the Round House in Chalk Farm, later at John Barons in Leeds and finally in Belfast.

He was a keen artist. Even in their small flat, his easel was always to be seen in the sitting room. I loved going there for tea.

In the summer holidays, my mother and I travelled to Liverpool. We were both excited to arrive at Euston Station. There were many people hurrying about. The great steam engines were an amazing sight, with the drivers and the men stoking up roaring fires in the furnaces. No one carried their own suitcases, which were heavy and cumbersome. A porter always took us to the right platform, carrying our suitcases on a little trolley, until we found a suitable compartment. A suitable compartment was a corner seat with your back to the engine. If you faced the engine, you could easily get smut blown into your eyes from the smoke, so that was to be avoided.

I remember on one occasion my mother could not find a suitable seat, so she called the Station Master, who arrived wearing his top hat. As a result, he then added an extra compartment to the train. Each compartment was sufficient for six people, and there was a passageway so that you could walk from one compartment to another. Once I was settled into the corner seat, my mother would then stand outside on the platform, together with many other passengers. I suppose she was watching the people going past.

I was always terrified that the train would suddenly shoot off and she would be left behind. However, once the guard blew his whistle and waved his green flag, she was safely inside, and the door shut.

She would then hand me a copy of a little children's paper called *The Rainbow*, and later, when I could read better, she would give me *Tiger Tim's Weekly*. Then, out would come the food: sandwiches and hard-boiled eggs.

When we arrived at Crewe, which was a big railway junction, everybody dashed out of the train to get a mug of tea. There were no refreshments on the train. Again, by a miracle, my mother got back into the train just in time and was not left behind – much to my relief.

When we arrived in Liverpool, we either went by tram or taxi to my Aunt Clara's large house in Croxteth Grove, Sefton Park.

My Aunt Clara had married Barron Stern, and they had four sons: Harold, a little younger than my cousin Marcus; then Edward; George, who was five years older than me; and baby Kenneth. We followed a certain routine in Liverpool: visiting the cemetery, meeting our cousins and attending Princes Road Shul on the Shabbat. The Reverend Frampton was the Minister for over forty years. I was dressed up in my best clothes to go to Shul, but as soon as we returned home my mother would say, 'Take off your good coat and clothes.'

We visited my mother's cousins, the family Myers. One of their family was an old lady who wore a pink patch over her eye. We visited Aunt Genette, who was married to Uncle Jack. They had a shop selling glassware of various kinds. I think it was in Walton Road. They were delighted to see us and before I left I was sent to see my Uncle in his office, where he gave me a golden sovereign. I duly gave it to my mother on the way home. In later years, this same Uncle Jack came to visit us in Norwood. I knew that he kept pigeons, and when he arrived he brought a carrier pigeon with him. Instead of telephoning home, he sent off the pigeon to say that he had arrived safely in London.

Chapter Five. Life with my Mother

We visited Dr Lowenthal, our family doctor, who originally had come from Germany. My mother set great store by his medical knowledge. Years later, he attended my wedding in Pretoria, South Africa.

After some days, the whole family went on a holiday to one of the lovely little seaside places on the other side of the River Mersey. Auntie Clara hired a house, probably for a month. We would all go down to the landing stage to catch the ferry. The landing stage was a very busy place in those days. There were boats from Ireland and boats from America, packed with bales of cotton, ready to go to the Manchester mills. The mouth of the River Mersey was a broad channel and the ferry that crossed the channel was a large vessel, called HMS *Daffodil*. This boat took part in the Second World War in the relief of soldiers from Dunkirk.

The HMS *Daffodil* took us across the Mersey to Birkenhead and then on to New Brighton, Hoylake and West Kirby. All picturesque little seaside resorts. The tunnel under the Mersey had not yet been built. It was possible for Uncle Barron to go across the water to his business in Liverpool every day and return to the rented house in the evening. On one occasion, we went on to Llandudno, which is in Wales, by the same boat. It seemed that all my memories were of lovely holidays, where it never rained, and the sun shone every day.

In the morning, we played happily on the beach and groups of children dug castles or big holes in the sand. Sometimes we paddled. I don't think anyone swam. My Aunt Clara and my mother never joined in these games, but sat on two deckchairs, doing embroidery. This seemed to be a tradition. In the afternoon, there was entertainment on the promenade – usually people dressed in Pierrot costumes who sang and danced. Children paid threepence and sat on two benches at the back to listen to the songs and enjoy the fun. You paid more for the more expensive seats in the front. When you sat on the back-bench, the other children in front of you leaned against your knees. That was something I did not like at all.

I told this to my cousin Harold, who was the eldest of the Stern boys and must have been about twelve years older than me, aged sixteen or seventeen. He treated me for an extra four pence so I could sit on a proper seat. Even in those days, Harold was keen on chemistry and gave me an exhibition of fireworks, which he made from bottles and bits of material.

My cousin Edward went to school in Birkenhead and I always thought how lucky he was because if there was a mist and the ferry did not go, then he had to miss the whole day of school. I remember my cousin Kenneth, who must have been about two or three, having a temper tantrum because he did not want to leave the beach. I stood by in amazement at such a display of temper.

I remember Uncle Barron sitting at the dinner table and saying to me, 'If you will sing a song, then I will give you a special doll that can open and shut its eyes and drink.' I thought how wonderful that would be. But I remember thinking how I would quite easily sing him a song without him promising me a doll. Shortly afterwards, he gave me a pretty china doll that I called *Isabelle*.

I had a repertoire of songs and poems that I would sing or recite to anybody who was willing to listen. I think my mother would make an excuse to stay on a little longer, but, of course, eventually we returned to London. I have no memory of the return journeys.

My Uncle Barron came originally as a young boy from Germany. My cousin Harold says his father was sent back there after his barmitzvah for further education both in religious and in general studies. His parents did not think that the standard was high enough in Liverpool.

Uncle Barron's business at first did very well, importing enamel-ware from Germany. The financial depression of the early thirties had a disastrous effect on his business and this affected him so much that ended his life in a most tragic way. After his sudden death, Aunt Clara and her son Edward started a successful business selling kitchenware, and her shops were called 'Kitchens'.

A few years later, the holidays in Liverpool came to an end. My cousin Harold graduated with a doctorate in Analytical Chemistry from Oxford University. He opened his own laboratory and helped to start firms in Israel, using his specialised knowledge of dyes. He was responsible for developing the material later used for hip replacements. Both George and Kenneth became captains of corvettes in the Second World War.

Growing Up

When I was about eight years old, Daddy Myer bought a Harley Davidson motor-bike with a side-car. My Aunt Esther would sit in the side-car and I would be strapped onto the pillion seat behind Daddy Myer. We would often drive to Brighton for the day. I don't remember much traffic on the road. I remember when it rained, we had to take shelter. There were no traffic lights or markings on the road. Daddy Myer was a member of the RAC (the Royal Automobile Club) and, along the route, RAC officers were stationed at strategic points. They would salute us as we went past.

In Brighton, we had a picnic on the beach and hired a bathing booth so we could change in privacy. Daddy Myer would try to teach me how to swim – in the freezing cold water. In the afternoon, we went to the cinema, where they both had a little doze, before setting off for home. In those days, they showed only silent movies.

Sometimes on a Saturday afternoon Auntie Esther, Daddy Myer and myself would walk to Tulse Hill to have tea with the Wolff family. The Wolff family lived in a very grand house. I think they had owned a famous pencil that was universally used called the 'Golden Sovereign'. There were two sisters; their brother played an organ. We were treated to a lovely tea with homemade cakes, everything baked on the premises by their cook.

Sometimes their niece, called Marie, who was my age, would come to tea with her mother and father. The two of us would give a performance: recitations and singing. Many years later, on their deaths, they left Marie their considerable fortune and, to my utter surprise, left me £100, which was a great deal of money in those days. It enabled me to do a lot of things, which I will tell you about later.

And so the years went by as I progressed through the school: Standard Two, then Three then Four (when I became rather naughty), until I reached Standard Six. Then I entered and won, much to my surprise, a London County Council Scholarship. This was a valuable prize because it meant free education at a High School, free books and even pocket money.

While I was in Standard Six, the whole class of girls went on holiday to Seaford. It was an unforgettable experience. We lived in attractive converted army huts, and we went out each day to places of interest, such as the mouth of the pretty little river of the Cuckmere, the castle at Lewes, and the sea-port of Newhaven.

When I was in Standard Six, the children from Norwood went to the Wembley Empire Exhibition. What a tremendous occasion! Before we set off, we were taught two new words. The first was the word 'rendezvous', which meant that if you got lost you were to wait at the door of any of the exhibitions until your group found you.

The second new word was 'toilet'. Apparently, 'lavatory' was not used, and this word 'toilet' was quite a new word for us. We were not allowed to go to the funfair, which disappointed us, but the rest of the exhibition we found interesting. We went down into a miniature coalmine. I am told that miners from Wales went to see it, as a home from home. The Canadian exhibition was of great interest. This included a miniature model of their great railway that I travelled on years later, when I went on holiday with Hans, from Calgary to Vancouver.

Chapter Six.

MY NEW SCHOOL. STREATHAM HILL HIGH SCHOOL

When I was eleven years old, I left the Norwood School and started at Streatham Hill High School. This school was part of the group of Girls' Public Day Schools Trust. It had been started about seventy years earlier so that girls could receive further education. It was fee-paying, but I had been fortunate enough to win a London County Council scholarship, and therefore we did not have to pay. I had to travel one stop on the railway from West Norwood to Streatham Hill station.

I walked to the school in Wavertree Road. I wore my new, green school uniform and matching blazer, with badge initialled S.H.H.S., a black felt hat with badge, black woollen stockings and a new small leather school-case with my initials K.P. on the front.

My interview with the Headmistress had taken place the previous term. Miss Gwatkin, the newly appointed Headmistress, had asked me to read some poetry. The interview had gone well.

When I arrived at the school, I was given a peg in the cloakroom for my outdoor clothes. The cloakrooms of the school were divided into four sections. My section of the cloakroom was called St. Patrick's. I was taken to my new form, Upper Three B, and shown to my desk.

Chapter Six. My New School. Streatham Hill High School

It was a single desk with a lid and ink well into which you dipped the nib of your pen.

I looked around at the girls who were sitting quietly in their places. I found the girls rather childish. I was already fairly tall and had recently started my periods, and, compared to the girls at Norwood, the girls here seemed very immature. That was not the worst point. It so happened that the Jewish holidays came in September and, coming from Norwood, which was very orthodox, I was obliged to take off every Jewish holiday from Rosh Hashanah to Succoth. It seemed that I missed at least one day every week during that September, which hindered my settling in.

I did not go into prayers, but remained upstairs in the Art Studio with four Catholic girls. There was one other Jewish girl, but she was much older and already in the sixth form, so I did not see her. When prayers were over, we came out on the balcony and listened to the announcements. To make matters worse, I stayed for school dinners and, as they were not kosher, I had to have special food, and so that was provided for me. This again made me feel different from the others. Finally, and this was the worst, every year the class studied one of Shakespeare's plays, and ours was *The Merchant of Venice*.

It seemed to me that every line had the word Jew in it, and I have hated the play ever since. All these points made me feel very much apart and different – after all, I had come from a completely Jewish environment and here I was out in the big world and feeling very isolated and unprotected after such a sheltered existence.

It never occurred to me to tell my family how I felt, and I just put up with it. I was pretty uncomfortable for at least six months of that year. I made friends, but they were not really my cup of tea.

At first, I thought the girls weren't really my sort. I suppose they came from very different and also sheltered backgrounds. There appeared to be no Jewish girls in the school. It was not until my second year that I met Beatrix (Trixie). We soon became close friends. I think we first became friendly because we shared the same surname: Kitty Pearson and Beatrix Pearson.

Trixie joined the school, in Lower IV, a year later. She also came with an LCC scholarship.

At first, she got on my nerves, because she seemed so happy, beaming and confident, compared to how insecure I felt; but soon we became great friends, sitting side by side throughout our schooldays. This made a great difference to me and I was much happier.

My new friend, Trixie, and I had no secrets from each other. She came to visit me in Norwood at least twice a month, and everybody liked her. I also went to stay with her. Her parents and family were working but struggling actors and actresses.

They went touring with theatre companies, and by the time I met them they had been in Australia and other parts of Britain. Her father was very much older than her mother. He was sixty and old enough to have been Trixie's grandfather. Trixie had a younger sister and the family lived in Kennington because it was cheap and near to town. It was what you would call today a red-light district.

Their flat consisted of two bedrooms – Trixie's mother and father slept in the one small room. In the other bedroom, Trixie shared a bed with her sister and her grandmother. I met many of her aunts and uncles and the talk was all about the theatre. If you went on a Monday, you would find the place full of sheets hanging on ropes in every bedroom, as there was no such thing as a laundrette in those days. Trixie's mother made all her clothes. I remember that she always said you can either have jam on your bread or butter – but not both. Nevertheless, Trixie was a very confident girl and ambitious. She was a conservative in her politics and said she wanted to be the Prime Minister. I thought this was ridiculous, as I had never thought a woman could become Prime Minister. But later she was proved right, as we had Mrs Thatcher here, Golda Meir in Israel and Indira Gandhi in India.

I was very fond of Trixie and of her family and it was good for me to see another way of life. They never seemed to know if they had money to buy food. I am so glad that my family never stopped me going there.

After that, I did make a few other friends. When we came to the sixth form, the room was set out differently. There were no desks and it did not look like a classroom. After the fifth form, many girls left and so the two parallel classes were joined together. This seemed more conducive to making new friends. Instead of going home by train every day, I started to walk with other girls to Tulse Hill and then caught the bus to Norwood. In this way, I became very friendly with three other girls.

I would stop for tea either with Betty Cazenova or Phyllis Winterbottom. And sometimes with Margaret Fisher. Fishy we called her. She was actually a Jewish girl, although she kept quiet about her Jewish background. I kept these four girls from Streatham as good friends for the rest of my life. Trixie later married a professor in Edinburgh. By the time I returned to England, they had retired and were living in Oxford. I kept in regular correspondence with Trixie. When I was living in South Africa and came on visits to England, I met with my old school friends, and when I returned to live in England I was able then to meet with Betty and Phyllis and Margaret regularly.

In this memoir I have looked for the first time, in a more critical way, at my time spent at Streatham Hill High School. During my school years, I took many things for granted. For example, I knew I was very good at sport. I was extremely good at netball. I usually won many of the running races and, because we had a tennis court at Norwood, I was a first-rate tennis player. For some reason, I was never encouraged in this ability at Streatham Hill. I was never encouraged to join any of the competitive teams. Perhaps they thought girls with scholarships would be better at schoolwork and not good at sport?

Most of all, I enjoyed the singing lessons and literature. Our class had a reputation for being good at Drama and I think, thanks to Trixie's influence, I always got a good acting part. Nevertheless, I felt different and this was understandable, because the school was made up almost entirely of white Church of England pupils. For example, one day the Headmistress announced that two girls from Egypt were coming to the school. She said that, because they had been in the sun so much, they would be browner than us, but we must not stare at them. Of course, we did all peer at them, because we were not accustomed to seeing any people of a different colour.

From the Lower Fifth, we had a very charismatic English teacher called Miss R. I enjoyed her lessons but, to my surprise, she failed me in an English examination. I had never failed before in an English test. I had always done very well in the subject. Shortly afterwards, the History teacher, Miss B, awarded me an A-plus for written work and she remarked that she did not agree or believe with the English teacher who had claimed that Jewish girls wrote in a peculiar and flowery manner. When I told this to my friend Betty Evans, the only other Jewish girl, as I've already mentioned, who was a few years older than me, Betty said, 'Oh, Miss R was very anti-Semitic.' At the time, I could not acknowledge that a teacher could have such a prejudice. I don't think I even knew what the term 'anti-Semitic' meant.

Although I was aware of feeling different, it did not occur to me that other people would see me as different, too. Any failures on my part I always attributed to my own inadequacies.

When Daddy Myer and Auntie Esther came to watch one of our plays, the German teacher, whose name was Miss W, whom I had never spoken to before, came up to me and said, 'Your father looks just like my own father.' It never occurred to me to invite her to speak to him. On another occasion, when Auntie Esther and my mother came to the Sports Day, dressed elegantly in summer dresses, I remember saying to them, 'On no account must you speak to the teachers.' One particular Open Day, it suddenly poured with rain, so imagine my amazement when I came upon my mother and my aunt having stripped off their dresses, in a room, together with Mademoiselle B, my French teacher, who had hung the wet dresses over the radiators to dry.

Why did I not invite any of the teachers back to Norwood? It never occurred to us. I saw teachers as something apart. Perhaps they might have been interested in visiting Norwood, and yet I held back from inviting them; but I did invite all my friends on many occasions.

When I went into the sixth form, I did not feel particularly successful, especially as I had not been chosen as a prefect – all of my friends had been chosen. However, when one prefect left the school willy-nilly, I was made one. Was this because of prejudice or my being rather outspoken? All my friends said it was disgusting that I was not chosen. I certainly was known to express liberal views and a dissatisfaction with the way that poor people were unsupported in our society, and I certainly gave expression to my political views during lessons.

AS TIME GOES BY

In the end, Miss R became my form teacher and I looked kindly on her. She suggested a lovely new edition of Jane Austen's collected works as my prize for distinction in History, which I cherish to this day.

Chapter Seven.

SCHOOL AND OUTINGS.

When I reached the sixth form, things improved considerably. Many girls took business courses at this stage, but a few of us continued with academic subjects. We had a new English teacher, who had just qualified at a university. Our French teacher, Mademoiselle Bosset, invited a small group of French pupils to tea every Sunday, which we enjoyed. Another pleasurable event was when I was in charge of the House choir. Before we left the school, our class invited the staff to a tea party which I arranged.

When I reached the sixth form, I developed more self-confidence, and this was helped by an improvement in my appearance. I was complimented on my improved appearance, and all this was greatly helped by the attractive dresses chosen by my mother.

During this time, Aunt Esther often obtained free tickets to theatres, and I enjoyed going to plays in the West End or visiting the cinema. We went to see plays by Bernard Shaw. Trixie and I went to the Old Vic, sitting up in the Gods for eight pence, and saw John Gielgud as Hamlet, Alec Guinness and Dame Sybil Thorndyke as Lady Macbeth. One day, on visiting the Royal Academy of Art, we saw John Gielgud looking with great interest at a portrait of Hamlet. Life became much more interesting and full of opportunities.

I mostly spent the weekends with my family. My Uncle Louis and his wife Annie had moved, with their little baby Ruth, from Wells Street to North London. Uncle Louis was now a designer for a firm that worked in the Round House in Camden. They bought a house in Wessex Gardens, Golders Green, and the house was only about two years old at the time. I thought it was attractive because it was so new.

When Ruth was five years old, she attended Wessex Gardens School, which was opposite to where they lived. I could go on the No 2 bus all the way from West Norwood to Golders Green for about one shilling. I often spent a Sunday or even a weekend with them. My mother and I no longer went up to Liverpool for holidays. I know that we went to Cliftonville for one holiday, the more exclusive part of Margate, and on another occasion we went with my Aunt Annie to Shanklin, on the Isle of Wight. But the most interesting holiday was my visit to Aix les Bain, in the Savoy district of France.

The journey in itself was an adventure. We had to go by train to Dover, boat to Calais, train to Paris, change trains and finally south to Aix les Bain. I was about fourteen years old at the time. It probably took about twelve hours, and what a different place from London! So, warm, so sunny – there were little cafés all along the roads, with trios playing tuneful music. Remember, there was no radio or wireless in those days. My mother and aunt took the waters and the baths. I remember in the evenings going into the grounds of the casino and watching through the windows the people dancing. We had two special outings during that holiday: first was in nearby Switzerland, where we went up to the top of Mont Blanc, on a funicular railway; and the second outing was to Lake Lucerne, where we took a boat trip.

On another occasion, I went with Uncle Louis and his wife Auntie Annie to Bognor Regis. Uncle Louis had bought a secondhand motor-car a few days before and he proposed to drive us by car. There was no need in those days to have any driving lessons or to pass any test. We set out early in the morning to avoid traffic on the road.

On the way, the hooter of the car broke, so Uncle Louis stopped and purchased a new one. My Auntie Annie held it in her hand and when Uncle Louis called out 'Hoot!', my Auntie Annie pressed the hooter. I know that I was given a pound for pocket money, a lot of money in those days, but the funny thing was I returned with the pound intact. Each time I wanted to buy something, I would say to Uncle Louis, 'It's no use breaking into this money for such a small sum.' This amused them. We had great fun on our outings and I remember we would play Ludo and Snap with cards, calling out instead of the word Snap – a long word like 'Constantinople thank you'!

Later, they moved to Roundhay in Leeds and I used to visit them for the Summer holidays. Uncle Louis was then in charge of an important company called *John Barons*. He designed coats and costumes which were then manufactured using various machines. Leeds was in those days a big city for the manufacture of clothes. Wherever we went, Uncle Louis would say, 'There's one of my coats. There's one of my costumes.'

At the weekends, we enjoyed visiting the Yorkshire moors.

We had a holiday travelling down the coast of Wales, going south from Aberdovey to a little farm outside Temby called Skrinkle. We climbed down a cliff and came to a beautiful sandy bay, which we had to ourselves. There was a large cave at one end and out in the bay we saw an island that had once been a monastery.

Now to return to school days. I did well in my final examination, obtaining a distinction in History. Nevertheless, I had no ambition to go to university; in fact, out of the whole class, only one girl – my friend Trixie – went on to Oxford. My friend Phyllis took a degree in Social Science. We all thought that this was to be a glorified cookery course, but it turned out to be something quite different. Today, girls would have been encouraged to continue their studies and go to university. Perhaps I could have taken a degree in History.

On the last day of term, my cousin Marcus kindly fetched me in his car in order to help me take all my books home. I left the school without a backward glance. I looked forward to starting my training as a teacher and going out into the real world – meeting young men and generally enjoying life.

Chapter Eight.

MY COUSIN MARCUS RETURNS FROM THE FIRST WORLD WAR

At this stage, I gradually saw less of my friends from Norwood – my friends like Annie, Rosie and Rosalind, who had left Norwood at the age of fifteen. As I lost touch with my Norwood friends, I became closer to the girls at Streatham Hill.

Meanwhile, at Norwood, new inventions were introduced, such as the wireless. It was fairly large and not a portable instrument, with knobs to turn on and off and to tune it in. There were a few wireless machines placed at strategic points around the orphanage. Some of the children were able to listen to the wireless and I know that I concentrated on learning the latest songs, which I considered very important.

My cousin Marcus, after being a prisoner-of-war in Germany during the First World War, came home and, like many soldiers, was deeply depressed. The War Office provided treatment for this condition. He was then about twenty years old. His brother Frank by then had left and was placed in the Manor House, Epsom – an institution for physically and mentally handicapped persons. Then, I had the bedroom to myself. As my bedroom had a nice fireplace and it was also very much a family sitting room, my Aunt Esther would sit in there.

Marcus was accepted at Caius College, Cambridge, where he took a degree in Mechanical Engineering. He did very well, gaining a triple first – that means getting first-class honours in three major courses, called Tripos. I remember going to see him in his study that he shared with an old friend, Mr. Stiff. This was when I was six or seven years old. Although, at first, there was a big difference in our ages, as I grew older the difference between us seemed less. Marcus always took a loving and brotherly interest in my welfare. He took me to the Queen's Hall, where the Promenade Concerts first started.

I got to know his friends from Cambridge. Later, some came to play a part in my life. There was Jack Rich, who was the editor of the *London Jewish Chronicle*, and later he came out to South Africa as secretary of the Johannesburg Jewish Board of Deputies. The Honourable Philip Samuel, a younger son of Viscount Samuel, invited me to many dances and allowed me to use his permanent seat at the Royal Albert Hall.

At Norwood, as I grew older I grew closer to the teachers and staff and came to see a different side of life in the orphanage. I saw things more from the teachers' point of view. I noticed how hard the staff worked and how little free time they had. There was a grass tennis court which I enjoyed using, and whenever I had free time I played tennis with members of the staff. Once a year, the staff had a dance in the dining-hall. There was a competition for who could do the best polka, and Auntie Esther and myself, both with partners, got through to the finals.

As I grew older, I would go regularly to the theatre. My Aunt Esther was given complimentary seats. She would say, 'Finish your homework and you can come with us,' which I did most speedily. We also went together to the Brixton Cinema, then called the Golden Domes. The films were in black and white with sound, and

Chapter Eight. My cousin Marcus returns from the First World War

this put an end to piano accompaniment. There was always one variety turn, as well as more popular music from the new electric Hammond organ which rose up in the cinema as the sound filled the hall. News reels, starting with a lion roaring, were part of the programme. They were produced by the Gaumont British Film Company. It was a family joke about these cinema visits – as Auntie Esther was never satisfied with the seats, and as soon as the lights went up, you'd find she had moved and her head was popping up either further forward or further back. She was not very good at geography, and when there was something on the screen she would add in her clear voice: 'Oh, yes, Le Havre – that's near Gibraltar.' Whereupon people sitting nearby would stiffen and correct her. This was nicknamed the *'Reed Geography'*.

I found the Talking Films more moving than the Silent ones, and sometimes I emerged red-eyed from watching the film. I remember a film about a boy called *Sonny Boy*.

When I was about eighteen years old, I visited Jack Rich's flat with Marcus and his friends. I remember they were all listening very intently to the wireless. I asked what it was about, and they said: 'There's a very terrible man in Germany who hopes to gain political power.' Fortunately, at this stage he was not elected. I, like many others, were very aware of the dangers of Hitler. I recall heated discussions in the Norwood staff dining room about this subject.

Chapter 9.

TEACHER TRAINING

In September 1931, I set out to attend the Furzedown College of Education, situated in Mitcham. I was to take a two-year training course and qualify as a teacher. The college was very large. Opposite was a big Secondary and Primary School. Once again it was an institution only for women and no men. The course that I took was called *The Theory and Practice of Education*, and it meant I could then teach in any of the State schools. I chose to qualify to teach children from nursery-school age through to Junior school.

I will describe some of the subjects we studied, but we were expected to have particular specialities. I chose English and Music. I do not think the English teaching was any better than the English that I had studied for Higher School Certificate at my former school. But the Music was a different matter. I could sight-read very well both tonic sol-fa and staff notation, but the rest of the subject was quite a challenge. Playing the piano, singing and teaching music in the schools went well. Other subjects of interest were Child Psychology, Education and the History of Education. But I found the Philosophy disappointing. I would have preferred to have studied the work of famous philosophers. Instead, we had the English philosopher Richard Stanley Peters, with lengthy discussions on the interpretations of words, which I found boring. Another subject which I found entertaining was called Art and Handwork.

We tried out weaving, clay modelling, sculpture, painting, sewing and knitting. We had to knit a pair of socks. Although I could knit, I never could turn the heel, so I gave the task to my Aunt Esther, who, after all, had knitted my socks since I was a child. She bought some white Silko and knitted a nice little pair of socks. She was very upset when the mark she got was only C-plus and was quite prepared to go up to the teacher to complain. But I stopped her. Apparently, most girls had little fancy patterns at the top and I found the whole episode quite funny.

In the first term, we visited a different school one day each week. This gave us an experience of different aspects of the educational system. Every term we were expected to go into a school and be responsible for one class for two weeks. In my first year I worked steadily, especially preparing the practical teaching, at which I always did well, coming from a family of teachers. I had already gained a wealth of experience by looking after the children at Norwood during the school holidays.

At Furzedown College we were put into a class and remained together throughout the course. We all got on well and were quite friendly. I became particularly friendly with another Jewish girl called Hilda Lewin, as well as Ethel King, known as Dink. Towards the end of this first year I met another Jewish girl called Sally Barnet, who had recently come from Buenos Aires. She did not do very well in the first year and she thought that was because she was too smartly dressed. The following year she appeared with horn-rimmed glasses and a dowdy dress and apparently her work improved. I went to stay with Sally Barnet, whose parents had bought a house in Croydon. She took me to the Croydon Shul, where she had already made friends with a suitable young man who, strangely enough, was distantly related to my family. He had a very handsome but rather dull friend. The four of us went out quite a bit together.

Summer Holidays

First, Betty Evans and I took the Norwood girls to the Caroline Barnet Hut in Seaford, which was owned by the Jews Free School. I was paid thirty shillings for this effort, and with this money I bought a portable gramophone. It was a box about two feet square – quite heavy, and you wound it up with a handle. It was made of black-painted wood. I was very proud of it. I played all kinds of records on it.

Daddy Myer had a brother-in-law called Moses Barratts, and he came from Manchester. He worked for a gramophone recording company and gave us a collection of records. We had the complete opera *Pagliacci* and Bizet's *Carmen*. Each album was very heavy and big. I learnt those operas in great detail and played them frequently. I also used to go and buy record singles made of a heavy material and I chose always the latest tunes. After winding up the machine and putting a needle in the arm, you carefully pulled it back and then placed it on the record and the music would start up.

When I went on holiday with Betty Casnov and Dink, I took my portable gramophone with me and we played songs and jazz. We once again visited my favourite place, Seaford, and we stayed in a little hotel on the seafront. We swam every day, played tennis in the afternoon and felt very grown-up. I remember that Marcus came down for the day and took all three of us out to tea. We thought he was very generous as he spent as much as thirty shillings on giving us this treat.

In my second year at Furzedown College, I continued to enjoy the practical teaching side of the course. I loved helping the children to learn to read, write and do Number work and to encourage them to work independently as far as possible. I know they enjoyed the stories I told them. For my part, I enjoyed particularly the musical side: singing, movement, listening and responding to music. Visiting lecturers gave me good reports, which was encouraging.

Chapter Ten.

SNEAKING OFF TO THE LOCARNO DANCE HALL

As far as my friends were concerned, I was increasingly friendly with Sally Barnet. She had taken Art as a special subject. She told me that she and her friend often visited the Locarno, a big Dance Hall near Streatham Hill Station.

'Why don't you come with us?' she said. 'It's good fun.'

I must have been eighteen years old, and this was the first time I concealed things from my family. So duly, one Tuesday, I set out to join them at the Locarno. I did not tell my Aunt where I was going as I know that she would not have approved, because it was a sort of free dance hall for everybody and anybody. I told her that I was going to study at Trixie's house and set out with my usual suitcase. Instead of having my books, my case contained an evening dress, shoes, handbag and a little make-up.

The Locarno was between Streatham Hill Station and the Streatham Theatre, so it was easy to get there. On the first floor was a tea-room, on the ground floor the box office and various cloakrooms. Down a flight of stairs there was a huge ballroom with a sprung floor, tables dotted around the dance-floor and on the raised platform an excellent large jazz band would play. The

Chapter Ten. Sneaking off to the Locarno Dance Hall

band consisted of at least four saxophones, violins, and a piano. It was a dance band.

The first thing I did was to go into the large ladies' cloakroom, where I met my two friends, changed into my evening dress in the toilet and handed in my suitcase containing my ordinary clothes to the assistant in the cloakroom, where you could leave belongings. I put the ticket in my handbag and we were off.

All the women wore long, fairly straight evening dresses made of different materials. The men wore ordinary suits with ties, not dinner jackets. No sooner had we arrived downstairs than someone came up to me and asked me if I would like to dance and I was away.

It was a joy to dance and the majority of the men were very good dancers. The dances were a foxtrot, slow foxtrot, waltz, an occasional polka and now and again that wonderful dance called the tango. Although I had learnt a long time ago to dance at school, I found that I just picked it up as I went along – it is quite an art to learn to follow your partner. There was no rowdiness or ill manners. There was no drinking of alcohol allowed and certainly no drugs. You could have tea or a soft drink and then you would sit at one of the tables to enjoy it. Women had to wait to be asked to dance, but luckily I had plenty of partners. I am sure that the young men wanted to meet girls, but I was mostly concerned with the joy and pleasure of dancing.

After this, I would go at least twice a week to the Locarno and I made a second evening dress out of curtain material. I had already started making my own clothes from patterns – called McCall's patterns, which were quite well-known. You could get the patterns in any size and I was the stock size. After a time, I met a very attractive man much older than myself. He was at least thirty, and he indeed was my first love. His name was Reggie M. I think he worked for the

Co-Op and he said he had been a choir boy at St. Paul's. After that I always met him to dance there. At one stage, Duke Ellington came across from America and he played with the band, and that was unforgettable. Reg and I then started to go to the cinema together and he introduced me to Studio 1 in Oxford Street.

I never told anyone and kept all of this a secret; but, of course, it could not go on for ever. Apparently, Sally Barnett's parents had accused me of having led their daughter astray!

As this came at the end of my teaching course, Sally was whisked away by her parents and I never saw her again. I do not know how Marcus found out about Reg M, but one day he showed me a letter that Reg had written to him. The writing was misspelt and showed a lack of education. Marcus said he wanted to meet him. How this came about I have no idea. My aunt and uncle never spoke to me about it and left the matter to Marcus, who said, in a rather humorous voice, pointing to this illiterate letter: 'Look at this, Kitty.'

I promised to turn over a new leaf, which eventually I did; but if I remember, that was only once I had left Norwood. Reg sent me a letter asking me to marry him and suggesting we meet to discuss it. I never replied, and I never went to meet him. To my shame, I was rather a snob and at that stage in my life I had no plans to get married – but he was really a very attractive young man.

Chapter Eleven.

MOVING TO WESTBOURNE TERRACE. MY FIRST TEACHING POST

Meanwhile, at College, I knew that I had passed the examinations and was a qualified teacher. I was interviewed by representatives from the London County Council (the LCC) and was placed on the list of first appointments. This meant that you could apply for posts within the London County Council area. This was an achievement, as only ten out of the whole College who applied were accepted.

Shortly after this, Miss Lloyd Evans, who was the principal of the College, had said there was a post going in West London at Addison Gardens School. The Headmistress said she wanted somebody who could play the piano, someone who did not need to keep her nose in the music book. This school was not far from where my mother was now running a little hotel, owned by the family in Westbourne Terrace, Bayswater. I went to visit the Headmistress, Mrs Bottroll, and she was pleased to accept my appointment, and so, towards the end of August, I left Norwood, where I had been since I was a baby of eighteen months old, and went to live with my mother at 122 Westbourne Terrace. Bayswater.

Westbourne Terrace was a long avenue that stretched from Kensington Gardens along to the end of a road which was parallel to Paddington Station. It was a wide, attractive road with terraces on either side – all Georgian houses. Each terrace was set back from the main road, approached by a side road.

The family owned two houses and half of another in this terrace, my mother being in charge. These houses had been converted into a private residential hotel. The entrance was at 122. Each house had a semi-basement, which was used as the kitchen, and on the ground floor was the dining room, a large attractive double room with a high ceiling, a hall with a staircase leading to the upper rooms. On the other side was my mother's sitting room. A private hotel meant that people were semi-permanent, and guests did not come and go. Most of the guests stayed permanently or for at least six months. They were expected to have some of their meals in the dining room. The food from the downstairs kitchen was brought up in a food lift and then served by two waitresses from a small kitchen. My mother gave me a very nice bedroom that was over the porch, so that I had a veranda with window boxes. I was very comfortable indeed. I think the two waitresses – who came, incidentally, from Ireland – were from the same family. They lived in the hotel, as did a male caretaker. But the cook and cleaners, who were permanently employed, came in daily.

We were near to the main road leading to Notting Hill Gate. In those days there were no traffic lights. At the crossroads, a policeman was stationed at busy times to direct the traffic.

My mother was responsible in every aspect for the management of the hotel. If you walked a few roads towards Queensway, passing similar but smaller terraces, you would reach the famous William Whitley's Store. This was the first General Store of its kind in London.

Chapter Eleven. Moving to Westbourne Terrace. My first Teaching Post

My mother would go every day to the huge Butcher's Department or Poultry Department. Whatever she purchased was then delivered to our hotel. When I accompanied her, we often visited the Dress, Coat and Fur Department. Everything could be purchased in this wonderful store. When the sales were on, my mother was in her element. I believe she once bought a beautiful fur coat for five pounds and won a prize for the best buy of the sales.

Addison Gardens School

In early September, I took the short bus ride to Notting Hill Gate, changed to another bus to the Olympia and Hammersmith, which brought me to the school in Addison Gardens.

The building – built as a result of the Education Act of 1830 – was of a particular design. It was a tall, large, rather forbidding structure. On the ground floor was the entrance for the infants. It was called Mixed Infants and referred to boys and girls in school together. The Girls' school was on the second floor and the Boys on the top floor. All three departments, including the Infant Department, were entirely separate.

There was a school hall and it was large enough to hold all the children for the assembly. The classrooms led off the Hall.

I was told it was the largest infant school in London. The grounds were asphalted. The Infant School had its own separate playground.

The children all lived in the immediate areas in crowded old tenement blocks, yet close by were some very expensive houses in the grander roads. The children that came to the school were from working-class families and not well off. Some were neatly dressed and seemed cared for; but others were very poor indeed. Some of them were sewn into their clothes at the beginning of winter. It was not unusual for children to have what we call a glue ear, and as there was no free medical care in those days, these children would be sent to the clinic, which was in a nearby hospital. The school was near the chief Postal Office of London, and many of the parents found work there.

Cadbury Hall was the headquarters of Joseph Lyon's numerous tearooms, which also provided employment, as did the Olympia and Hammersmith shopping area. The children all came from round about and only very occasionally we might have some children on a temporary basis, when their parents were working in the Circus at Olympia.

There were ten women members of staff, including myself in the Infants School, as well as the Headmistress. The school had a resident, male caretaker. On my first day, Mrs Bottrill, the Headmistress, took me to my class. It was one large room divided into three tiers which were raised so that the children at the back could see. The double desks accommodated two children sitting side by side. I remember looking at them quite fondly, thinking this is my first class. It was a very hot day and the children were sitting silently at their desks, looking at me with interest. The children were aged between six and six and a half. I had a register in front of me with their names, and no sooner had I finished calling out their names, when the teacher from next door came in to shake my hand. She turned to the children and said: 'Now, if any child gives Miss Pearson any trouble, send them straight to me.'

There was not a peep out of any child, and looking at the timetable I commenced the day's routine. Two other teachers came during the next half an hour and introduced themselves to me and said the same thing, warning any child thinking of giving any trouble that they would be sent straight to her classroom.

I have never had trouble with discipline and always found children responsive. But, of course, the teachers were not to know, and they meant kindly. The first morning, when school closed, I dashed off to have lunch at a Lyons Tea Shop in Hammersmith's Broadway, but when I came back one of the staff said: 'Where were you? We always have our lunch together in the staff room.' After that, I had my lunch with them. The staff room was all rather ordinary and unattractive. It had a table large enough for us to sit around, a gas cooker and a miserable, triangular sink-cum-wash basin. When we asked if we could have better washing facilities, we were told that we could only have that if our wash basin was broken.

In desperation, we tried to break it with a hammer as it was a shocking, miserable little thing for all the teachers to use to wash their hands and clean the dishes.

Now a word about the staff: I was very fortunate to be a member of this group of teachers. The Headmistress, Mrs Bottrill, was a capable, intelligent, tactful and amusing person. Maybe it was her leadership that made everyone work so happily together. The staff were all experienced teachers. In those days you were not allowed to teach if you were married, but three of the staff were married before this inhibiting Act was introduced. We all sat in set places around the table after cooking our lunch and the conversation was interesting and cheerful.

I remember it was the time when the Prince of Wales was meeting Mrs Simpson and the English papers did not mention it, but one of the staff had got hold of a paper from America, which we discussed with great interest. I can see them still sitting round the table: Miss Hankin, Miss Smith and Miss Dunbabbin on one side, myself at the end, then Miss Pusey, Miss Berden, Miss Knight and Miss Baldwin. My mother always gave me an interesting lunch prepared by our cook and sometimes I just had to warm it up. I remember Miss

Pusey saying to me once, 'You are lucky having such an easy life with your food all prepared for you'; and Miss Hankin said, 'Anyone who works here does not have an easy life.'

The year was 1931 or 1932. They were all much older than me. The nearest in age to me was Miss Knight, who was about twenty-eight years old. I can only say how very kind, helpful and pleasant they all were.

I did not stay with my first class for more than a month, but was transferred to the new Admission class. Here there were a large number of children. The entrance led directly to my classroom. I was rather surprised to have such a large number of children in my charge. There were no assistants in those days. I remember quite early on looking out of the window and seeing a child wandering by itself in the street. I thought 'My God, a child has wandered off,' and I dashed into the road and brought the little boy back. Five minutes later, a distraught mother appeared in the room and claimed him. He was not one of the children in my class, after all.

Now about the school programme. Three or four mornings a week there would be a general assembly in the Big Hall. I would march my children into the Hall and see that they were seated cross-legged on the floor, in front of a small platform, where Mrs Bottrill would be waiting. I then went to the piano and played a few cheerful marches as the rest of the children joined us for the school assembly. Mrs Bottrill would then make a few announcements. She would tell us who had won 'the banner'. I really didn't know what that meant at first. But, apparently, it meant the class with the least number of absentees and the best attendance. Incidentally, attendance was a high priority. We had to record every week the children in our class who were absent. This information was given to a full-time attendance officer who would follow up cases.

Chapter Eleven. Moving to Westbourne Terrace. My first Teaching Post

At the Assembly we sang a few semi-religious songs written in a book by Carey Bonner. Songs such as *Butterflies are Pretty Things* or *God made little Robins*. On the days when we did not have assembly, teachers were expected to carry out, first thing in the morning, a semi-religious lesson period. This consisted of the following: Arranging flowers and 'handkerchief drill'. Remember, there were no tissues in those days, and each child had to produce a proper handkerchief, which they usually waved about, probably transmitting germs everywhere. We then sang a few hymns, which were followed by stories from the Bible. One of the hymns which always amused me was

> 'Jesus bids us shine with a clear, clear light,
> Like a little candle burning in the night,
> In this world of darkness, we must shine,
> You in your small corner (*pointing to me*)
> And I in mine (*pointing to themselves*).'

It's interesting to note that although everyone knew that I was Jewish, yet nobody questioned my ability to teach religion. When it came to Bible stories, I tried to make the story of Moses in the bulrushes and Noah with his ark and the flood continue as long as possible. I didn't know the story of baby Jesus at that stage.

The curriculum was progressive for those times, with an emphasis given to understanding the value of numbers before children began theoretical arithmetic. There was a time when the children were able to work individually with various suitable activities such as playing with cards, threading beads, playing dominoes, ludo and other suitable activities, as well as using the apparatus we had made to help them.

We taught Reading by combining various teaching methods: a phonetic approach and what is called the Look and Say Method.

We saw reading as not an isolated subject but part of all learning. The idea we favoured was that children were encouraged to learn to read for its own sake, for the meaning of what they read, not a parroting of words.

In my first term, as Christmas approached, we had a staff meeting. Mrs Bottrill told us about a school concert she had attended locally. Each child held a tulip and sang a popular song, '*Tiptoe through the tulips*'. Then we went on to discuss our Christmas party. Each class made a Christmas pudding and certain noble teachers volunteered to cook these puddings in their own homes. Mrs Bottrill then went on to mention a new style of Christmas decorations that she wanted to see in the classrooms.

I was a bit bewildered by this and asked Miss Smith how she was going to manage this new type of decoration. She smiled and said to me, 'I shall do the same as usual.' '*The same as usual*' meant the children made little paper chains, looped around the classroom, and we pinned up cheerful Christmas pictures on the walls. When it was time for the Christmas puddings, I had to give each child a little mound of ingredients on each desk and they mixed them up with their hands (I have no idea if they washed their hands first or not). Everything was put into a basin and every child had a chance to stir the pudding. Each child seemed to enjoy this, but it put me off my food for a few days.

When the Christmas party came, I was amazed to see how children enjoyed eating plain bread and butter as well as the Christmas pudding and other party food. And soon the first term ended. I enjoyed my work at the school, as well as making good use of my free time at weekends.

Chapter Eleven. Moving to Westbourne Terrace. My first Teaching Post

New Responsibilities

Daddy Myer had been at school in Liverpool with the Reverend Walter Levine. Together, they arranged for me to teach children at the Bayswater Shul on a Sunday morning. The children were quite rowdy and were probably as unenthusiastic as I was on a Sunday morning to be studying Hebrew. When I was accompanying the singing at Addison Gardens School, Mrs Bottrill said, 'Play a little faster, dear'; but in contrast, Walter Levine in the Bayswater Hebrew School said, 'Play slower, slower.' That was when I was playing *Adom Alom*.

After some time, I discontinued teaching Hebrew as I preferred to have my Sundays free.

My salary as a full-time teacher was fifteen pounds a month. These were times of the Depression and salaries had been cut back, but I thought the fifteen pounds was splendid and I managed on it quite well. I gave my mother thirty shillings (£1.50) a month, which she saved for me (although I didn't know it at the time), and I was free to spend the rest as I wished. I made a lot of my own clothes from paper patterns, and whatever was left I spent.

A very attractive new unit was completed in the following term at Addison Gardens School. Children who were five years old were admitted to this unit. The building had its own entrance, cloakroom, toilets and classroom. I was put in charge. In the afternoons, each child had their own stretcher-bed, where they had their rest. Many fell asleep. About this time, a Labour Government introduced free milk and the publicity about this introduction was filmed at our school. The children were given a small bottle of milk with a straw they inserted in the lid. The children certainly relished this drink and looked forward to the time of day when they would sit and drink it. Free milk continued until years later, in the eighties, when Mrs

Thatcher, who became Prime Minister, stopped it. People called her *Mrs Thatcher – Milk Snatcher.*

Remember, all children went home at lunch time. The hours were 8.50am to 12 noon and 2pm to 4pm in the afternoon. On occasions, the School Inspector would arrive unannounced. Mrs Bottrill had a secret sign, which she sent around to every teacher to warn them that the Inspector was present. The warning took the form of a child being sent from class to class carrying a ruler. On the whole, the Inspectors were quite positive and helpful. As I was a newly qualified teacher, they had to observe me carefully, before I was finally accepted by the authorities.

Chapter Twelve.

GOING TO DANCES. MEETING HANS

Meanwhile, I enjoyed going to live with my mother in Westbourne Terrace. I had a very lovely bedroom with a veranda over the front porch. We were near Kensington Gardens, near attractive shops, theatres, cinemas and concert halls. I was invited to many dances. I enjoyed it all and rarely stayed at home, even during the week. On a Sunday it was lovely to go into the country on the Greenline bus and walk with a group of friends. There were two nearby local synagogues that arranged dances for young people: the St Petersburg Place and the Bayswater Synagogue. The St Petersburg Place Shul was remarkable in that it was a replica of the Princes Road Shul in Liverpool. The Samuels (later Viscount Samuel), when they came to London, had suggested this.

These dances were held at the Grosvenor Hotel or the newly built Dorchester Hotel. All proceeds went to charity and although I didn't have such good dances as at the Locarno Streatham, I met many quite attractive young men.

A Norwood old boy, Sam Harbour, had become Box Office Manager at the Coliseum, where he lived with his wife in a flat on the first floor. He saw to it that we always had wonderful seats for the American musicals. Much later, when I came on a visit from South

Africa with my little son David, aged about six, he gave me front-row Dress Circle seats to see *Annie Get Your Gun*.

I soon met a number of young men and went out with them, one of whom made a marriage proposal to me on the bridge in beautiful St James's Park. However, I was not considering getting married at this stage in my life, but rather wanted to enjoy myself. That summer I went with my college friend Dink by boat from the Port of London to the Port of Leith in Scotland. It took one night and a day. I even had a little romance on the way up. We travelled from Port of Leith to The Trossachs, staying at youth hostels. This is 1933. I had left my spectacles on the boat and a young man from the boat discovered where I was and brought them to me.

The youth hostels were very inexpensive and had only just started in England and Scotland. You had to bring a knife, fork and spoon and a sleeping bag and you paid about 2/6d (12.5p) for each night. The people spoke English with such a broad Scottish accent that it was hard to understand what they said. As a result of this, I heard a young man remark, 'These English girls can only smile but say nothing.'

To wander around Loch Lomond was wonderful. One thing I remember clearly: on the return journey, we were in a bus, discussing how we would manage with our last five shillings. Either to have breakfast and walk to Port of Leith or to do without breakfast and ride to the port. A very quietly spoken lady leaned forward and said, 'Please, take these five shillings.' When we protested, she said this was a little bit of Scottish hospitality, and so we accepted.

Finally, in 1934 I celebrated my 21st birthday. My mother removed the dining room furniture and we held a dance, with a small trio, and refreshments. I invited friends to celebrate the occasion. I already had the key of the door before this time.

Chapter Twelve. Going to Dances. Meeting Hans

On looking back at what has already been written, I am surprised how little I was concerned with the serious situation unfolding in Europe. Of course, I was aware of what was going on. I remember that my friend Betty Evans had met a charming man who was a Jewish refugee from South Germany. He was a printer and knew all about colour printing. There was little known of this in England at that time and so a firm in Watford gave him a permanent job. I think they printed magazines. He was one of the lucky ones. I remember, also, at a discussion at the staff table when Hitler had made his first 'Putsch' and one of the staff said, 'For goodness sake, let him have it. We don't want to go to war. We have had enough war.'

When I was twenty-one, Marcus's friend Jack Rich, at that time editor of the *Jewish Chronicle*, wanted to give me a twenty-first birthday present, and we went to a print shop. He said, 'Any picture you like, except one that has been printed in Germany.' That also brought the situation home to me. I suppose at the time I was too busy enjoying myself, living an enjoyable life in the centre of London. However, this would shortly change.

I meet Hans

One afternoon, after Pesach in 1934, when I returned from teaching at Addison Gardens, my mother said that our friend, the Reverend Walter Levine, had left me two tickets for a dance. It was unusual for me to get tickets like this. I usually went with a group arranged by the Honourable Philip Samuel, a great friend of my cousin, Marcus. He often arranged a party to go to a dance in aid of his favourite charity. This was different, because I was given two tickets. I would never say no to a dance, so I rang up my friend Harry M, and he was very willing to come with me. Harry was, I think, very much in love with me and we were going out regularly.

The dance was in the middle of the week at The Connaught Rooms. It was a popular place for Jewish events. I didn't put myself out particularly as it was rather short notice, but Harry and I set forth together for the dance hall. There was a lively little orchestra in the large ballroom. We found an empty table and sat together. After a few dances, the orchestra announced that there would be 'A Paul Jones'. This was a special dance, where everybody joined in together. The women made a circle holding hands and the men made another circle on the outside. The orchestra then played the *Paul Jones* tune, which everyone knew. When the music stopped, you danced with whoever was facing you. If there was nobody facing you, you were unlucky.

Then it happened – I stopped opposite two men. One was rather small and the other taller. I noted that the taller one had a dinner jacket that was a little bit small for him, as if he had grown out of it. But he looked rather nice, so I chose him. The orchestra started playing a new dance, which happened to be a tango. I was impressed with my partner, who seemed to know a lot of complicated tango steps. After a little while, the dance continued with other partners. The *Paul Jones* was always a good chance to meet new people.

After the dance, Harry and I went back to sit at our table. When the music started up again, almost immediately this same young man rushed up to me and asked me to dance again. I was too astonished to say no. And then we danced again. I thought he was rather attractive, and when he asked me for my telephone number I gave it to him: Paddington 5044.

The very next day he rang me up and asked me if I would like to have a meal in his apartment. I was very impressed with the word 'apartment'. I imagined some palatial flat somewhere. We met at Great Portland Street tube station and went for a walk in the beautiful Regent's Park. Somehow, we arrived at a small market,

Chapter Twelve. Going to Dances. Meeting Hans

where Hans did a little shopping. And then we returned to his house in Albany Street, which was either number 51 or 53. I'm not quite sure. He introduced me to his landlady, Miss Tarlton, and took me upstairs to a room where he lived on the first floor. This was quite a new experience for me. I had never been to a young man's room like that before because most of the young men I knew still lived at home with their parents.

He put money in the gas stove to make it work, put a pot on the little gas ring and boiled some haddock for our supper. I don't remember if we had anything else. And then he told me a little about himself. He talked about his mother Lottie, who had died just before he took his final school exams.

His name was Hans Freund and he came from Germany. He lived in Berlin with his father. He had recently obtained his Doctorate at Göttingen University. He had studied Germanistics (Philology, Philosophy and Literature), and after that he came to England to improve his English, where he had relations. He had studied at University College London. He then returned to Germany, but when Hitler came to power on 30th January 1933, his father said, 'This man can't last. But you had better go back to London for the time being.' He packed a small suitcase and returned to London. He was twenty-three years old.

He invited me to go out the following Sunday for a walk in the country. I suggested inviting Betty Evans and her boyfriend Rudy Behr, from south Germany, to join us. During the week, Hans wrote to say he would prefer if we went by ourselves. The following Sunday, we set out on a walk that he obviously knew well. I remember suggesting we follow another path, but he said, 'Oh, no. You can get completely lost in England,' and he wanted to stick to the path he knew. We continued until we reached a tea room which he had already told me about. For 2/6d a head you could get a full tea: bread and butter, cakes and scones. After this delicious tea, we returned home. I must say I liked him very much indeed. Soon after this, I intended to go away for the Whitsun Bank Holiday weekend with my cousin Marcus and his friends. We planned to go to Seaford, to the old-fashioned beach hotel on the seafront. I asked Hans if he would like to join us, but he said it was not possible. It never occurred to me that he couldn't afford it. He may have had other reasons. It was a lovely weekend and I remember walking up the wonderful Seaford Head before breakfast – no joke to climb and from where you could look across the downs to the Cuckmere River with the white cliffs beyond, known as the Seven Sisters.

Myer Kaye, Headmaster of Norwood in his TB (Thompson Bros) cycle car, a three wheeler.

I am sitting in a class in Norwood School.

1936 Hans and his father taken before Hans left for South Africa.

Hans joins the South African forces, to fight with the Allied Army in North Africa.

When I was twenty-one.

10.12.36 Our Wedding day in Pretoria.

Chapter Thirteen.

HANS LEAVES FOR SOUTH AFRICA

After this, Hans and I met often. He introduced me to his cousin Ernie in a little pub near to Regent's Park, in Albany Street, called, strangely enough, *The Cape of Good Hope*. This was the first time I had been in a London pub, although in the country it was a different matter. At that time Ernie was a professional musician. He played the violin in a trio at one of the Lyons' two corner houses. Later, we went to have tea there and Ernie, on seeing us, immediately gave a most polished performance of a violin concerto. Another time, Ernie and his older brother Henry took us to see a shop which they had rented, where they were going to sell antique furniture.

Years later, the two brothers became very successful and opened a large showroom called The Pelham Antique Galleries near South Kensington tube station. It became quite famous in the world of antiques. Daddy Myer, who was always interested in antique furniture, bought furniture from them.

Much later, when we came to Britain on holiday from South Africa, Henry, who had become Chairman of the Antique Dealers Association, took me, together with his wife Lily, to see the antique fair at Grosvenor House. Lily told all the dealers that I was a cousin from South Africa. I remember that she gave me a photograph of Henry shaking hands with the Queen.

Hans took me to see Ernie's father, Jack, who owned a house in Fitzroy Square. Jack had been orphaned as a boy in Poland and Hans' grandmother had taken him in and looked after him in Berlin.

When Jack was fourteen, he came to England and studied the specialised craft of painting flowers on furniture, which was very fashionable at that time. I remember seeing their beautiful grand piano that he had painted. Jack settled down here and prospered.

Gradually, Hans told me more about himself. At first, his father was able to send him money from Germany, but later this became illegal. University College was very good to Hans: it offered him the chance to teach classes in German conversation. This enabled him to stay in England. But the University did not pay him. Times were very difficult for the refugees because there was a depression in England and it was hard for them to get work and therefore many could not stay in Britain and searched for work in other countries. Hans managed to survive because a man whose name I have forgotten, who imported toys from Germany, paid him out of his own pocket for doing his translations. It was only bits of part-time work.

Hans had lost his mother five years previously, when he was eighteen. She had died of pneumonia, which was a very serious illness in those days. She had been a very beautiful woman, with her dark red hair. She was a first-class pianist and played some of Beethoven's piano concertos. Hans had inherited her red hair, but it was of a lighter shade. My daughter Erica has inherited the same gene and also has red hair.

Hans had two uncles who were rabbis, one in Hanover and the other in Berlin. His father, David, was the only one who went into business. He had a big shop in Berlin, where they sold linen, materials for curtains and general haberdashery items.

His uncle in Hanover was the rabbi of the very large and imposing synagogue. He was forced to watch as the Nazis burnt down the Hanover Synagogue. Many years later, after the war, they rebuilt the synagogue as a token of repentance and to try and make good this cruel act. The new synagogue was modern and much smaller. They put up a memorial for Hans' uncle and called the street *Freund Allee*. His other uncle was a Community Rabbi (Geminedes Rebbiner), who eventually went to live in Jerusalem. He was a rabbi in Berlin at the same time as the renowned Rabbi Leo Beck.

On one occasion, Hans took me to Woburn House, which was a centre for German refugees, where they learnt English and were helped in every possible way. We attended a concert performed by very well-known people from Germany. Hans kept telling me that these performers were some of Germany's greatest songwriters, pianists and musicians. It was truly a lovely concert, but a very sad occasion to think that these people were forced to flee from their country.

I told Hans that I had lived at the Jewish orphanage at West Norwood with my aunt and uncle and he said, 'Oh, I could have gone there for Pesach with Mrs Israel Abrahams.' She was the daughter of the Reverend Singer, who compiled the Singer's Prayer Book and was herself a very charming person. She had become a widow, and she lived in West End Lane, opposite the home of Cecil Roth, the well-known Jewish historian.

'What a pity,' I said. 'We might have met much earlier.'

'Oh, no!' he said. 'If I had met you there, I would never have had the nerve to ask you out.'

Mrs IA, as we called her, seemed determined for us to meet, and she invited me to tea one day and introduced me to Hans. I did not let on that I already knew him. So we bowed formally to each other and later met up again in the evening and went out.

There were two memorable events that I remember. The first was a visit to the open-air theatre at Regent's Park. It had not been open for very long. I think at that time it was held where the cafe is today. It was a broad amphitheatre with chairs arranged in rows in a large semi-circle. It was a beautiful summer evening. I will never forget sitting there with Hans, surrounded by tall trees, the sun setting and the birds singing their evening chorus.

The play was my favourite, 'A Midsummer Night's Dream'. There is something magical about seeing Shakespeare performed in the open air and hearing beautiful lines of the play.

'I know a bank where on the wild thyme grows' or *'and there the snake throws her enamelled skin weed wide enough to wrap a fairy in'*, or when Bottom is given the donkey's head: *'Oh, Bottom, thou art translated'*.

The play ended with Mendelssohn's well-known and well-loved incidental music and the final words were quoted; *'If we mortals have offended, think but this and all is mended.'* As we walked home through the closed and silent park, we were not offended – we were enchanted.

On another occasion, Hans took me to the Queen's Hall to hear his favourite Beethoven's 5th Symphony. He managed to find the record of this piece of music, which in those days was a large round heavy disc. He put a label on it to remind me that he had given it to me as a date to remember. However, the situation was very difficult for Hans. He felt very insecure in London because, at the whim of the Home Office, he could be asked to leave the country.

Chapter Thirteen. Hans leaves for South Africa

And the second priority was to get his father out of Germany, out of a fearful situation.

For these reasons, he was applying everywhere in the world in the hope of finding employment. At one stage, when he had to go and renew his visa, he took me with him to Petit France, in London, just in case he needed help. But, fortunately, this time all went well, and he was very relieved. At this time, he met a business man from Johannesburg, South Africa, who offered him a post in the CTC Bazaars, a very large store, part of a chain of general stores. This meant he could leave Britain with all the visa problems and settle more safely in South Africa.

This was a big decision and Hans accepted it. Before Hans left for South Africa, his father came for two weeks to visit him. We met – probably at Woburn House – and I thought that Hans looked very like his father, although his father David was much shorter. A few days later, as I was walking in Bloomsbury, I heard someone call 'Kitty'. It was Hans' father. We looked at each other and I smiled at him and looked meaningfully into his face; but, unfortunately, he spoke no English and I knew no German. He looked at me very seriously and I have never forgotten this moving occasion.

Before Hans was due to leave, I at last invited him to my home and we had a small farewell party. I thought it was an opportunity for my family to meet him and also a chance to introduce him to my mother. Marcus was there, and I think my cousin Harold, as well as Ernie, who brought along his violin, and my friend Phyllis, who was a better pianist than me. We had some good music and my mother, as ever, produced delicious food.

The time arrived for Hans to leave England. The committee at Woburn House bought him a ticket to Southampton and also a one-way ticket on the Union Castle Line to Cape Town. In addition, they paid for the train fare for the long journey from Cape Town to Johannesburg. He told me that he needed £50, which he had to show to the authorities in South Africa before they would allow him to disembark. He asked me if I would lend him this money, as he was not sure if he would need additional money. Of course I agreed, as I had the £100 that Miss Woolf had left me in her will. I thought at the time what a changed situation for him. He was an only son from a comfortably well-off family, and I am sure he had never lacked money in the past. What a different situation for him now.

The time came for him to leave. On his last night in England, he was staying in a hotel, where I went to join him. To my surprise, his clothes were strewn all over the place. He had not yet packed. Even when the taxi was at the door, he was still putting his things into the suitcases. I suppose when the time came to leave it was hard for him to face it, and I remember that for the rest of his life Hans always found it difficult to pack, even for a holiday. He found packing and leaving stressful.

Eventually, we arrived at Victoria Station in time for the boat-train to Southampton. I was outwardly calm, but inwardly overwhelmed. I don't know how to describe it. Hans was going away on a long journey to the other end of the world. Remember, in those days there was only the boat to take you to South Africa, and even a letter took a fortnight.

We reached Southampton Docks and went on board. Strangely enough, although I was born in Liverpool, I had never been on a big liner. All the same, I could see this was an old boat and Hans' berth was very crowded, with six in the cabin. I don't think there was a porthole. His room opened out onto the dining room, which had benches to sit on instead of chairs. All too soon came an announcement to say that visitors must leave the boat, which I did. I stood with a little group on the quayside while the band played

God Save the King. Hans stood looking down at me and, as the boat slowly moved out, tears streamed down my face. A seaman in the group tried to cheer me up, I suppose, and said in a loud voice, 'Hope someone cries for me when I leave!' But it didn't help me. There is nothing so difficult as seeing a boat leave.

A train rushes out of the station, but a boat goes away slowly. At first, there was just a space of water between the boat and the quayside. And slowly the faces began to disappear and slowly the boat went further and further away, beyond the horizon, until it disappeared from view. I returned by train to Victoria, where the newspaper vendors had posters announcing: 'The King is gravely ill.'

Chapter Fourteen.

LETTERS FROM SOUTH AFRICA. SAD NEWS

Four weeks later, I received my first letter from Hans. It was a long letter written during the two weeks that he had been on the boat. It was a loving letter, but I remember he mentioned one incident. The news was announced that King George V had died on 20th January 1936. A memorial service was held on the boat to commemorate the King's death.

Hans attended the service and a passenger thanked him. The passenger, realising he was a foreigner, appreciated how Hans wished to join them in paying respects.

As soon as the boat left, I wrote a short letter to Hans, thinking that the mail boat might arrive before he got to Cape Town. This was the case and, on 30th January 1936, Hans arrived in South Africa. I had addressed the letter to a Mrs Wolf, the wife of an Ear, Nose and Throat specialist, the sister of Miss Chapman, who was to arrange Hans' passage to Johannesburg. Hans said that she met the boat and took him to her home in Sea Point, a suburb of Cape Town. While he was there, my letter arrived. He wrote back to me a short letter in reply, because Mrs Wolf was about to take him to the train for the long journey he was to make from Cape Town to Johannesburg. This rail trip was to take two days and two nights. Hans promised

Chapter Fourteen. Letters from South Africa. Sad News

to write again when he arrived in Johannesburg, and so the first of our many letters were exchanged.

His next letter came after four weeks. He had a lot to tell me. Firstly, he was met at Johannesburg station by his father's old friend, Willy Shapiro. A year before, Willy had helped Hans' father sell his business in Berlin. The shop was a big one, selling linen and materials in 33 Bad Strasse. Hitler's edicts had meant people stopped buying from his father's shop, and after 'Kristallnacht', his father held a closing-down sale. Hans had described to me how his father stood at the door of the shop at the closing-down sale and said to his old customers, 'Well, you come now ... but where were you when I needed you?'

His father had previously given up their flat above the shop where Hans had been born in 1910. He had moved into two rented rooms somewhere near his other relations in Berlin. Willy Shapiro had, by then, left Germany and opened his own business in Germiston, which was along the reef near Johannesburg. After Willy had greeted Hans, he said to him, 'Do you see anything strange about my clothing?'

'Yes,' said Hans. 'One of your button holes is torn and it's a sign of mourning.'

'I'm afraid I have to tell you that your father died while you were on the boat. Your father collapsed in the street and was taken to the Jewish hospital, where he died.'

Hans wrote that he had only been in Johannesburg for two weeks, but even after this short time he was sure that his father would have been able to make a good life for himself in South Africa. He had received his last letter from his father begging him 'to get me out of this hell as soon as possible'.

Hans then went on to tell me that he had started work with the CTC Bazaars, but not in the post that he had anticipated. The manager had told him that as soon as there was a better job available, he would be offered it; but, in the meantime, he was to work in the CTC Bazaars' large warehouse. He had to open crates with goods arriving from Europe. He had to list the goods enclosed and keep a record of what was taken out of the storeroom. That was the contents of this first long letter, and although he did not complain, it was clearly a very sad start to his new life.

Life in London Continues

I continued to live with my mother. Although we still had quite a few years left on the lease, the owners were planning to rebuild the entire terrace. This actually never happened, because the Second World War intervened, but we weren't to know that at the time. My mother and the family started to look for another suitable small hotel. They found a hotel in Inverness Terrace, which was practically opposite Kensington Gardens.

It was known as a private hotel where people lived on a fairly permanent basis, having meals in the public dining room whenever it suited them. The people who lived there were mostly ladies working in London. Many were very interesting people. This private hotel, called Sayers Court, consisted of two and a half houses. This house was quite similar to the one in Westbourne Terrace, but was more substantial. It needed redecoration and new furniture for some of the rooms.

All I had to do was cross the road and walk straight into beautiful Kensington Gardens. It was easy to go to my school on a bus all the way to Addison Gardens. In the next road, parallel to Inverness Terrace, was Queensway, with the famous Whitley's Department Store, where

Chapter Fourteen. Letters from South Africa. Sad News

you could buy everything, whether it be food or clothes. My mother was in her element visiting Whitley's every day, ordering the food and never failing to keep her eye on the clothes departments. The tube and the bus were close at hand and took you into the West End.

My cousin Harold and his younger brother George lived in the mews opposite our house. I think it was in Inverness Terrace that we heard Richard Tauber's magnificent voice ring out from the other side of the mews. We learnt he was singing for a friend who lived there.

About this time, Daddy Myer and Auntie Esther retired from the Norwood Orphanage after having been in charge there for the last twenty-five years.

They went to view various flats to rent, all of which were on the other side of the park in Palace Gate.

'I begged your aunt to let us buy one of the new flats that were being built in Kensington, but she preferred one of these old large flats,' said Daddy Myer.

This, of course, was a great mistake, as prices eventually rose beyond all bounds. It taught me a lesson, and we always bought our home as soon as it was possible.

While we lived at Norwood, we went to our own shul in the orphanage. Now we had to decide which synagogue to join, and one that was near to where we lived. Daddy Myer made the decision. He felt that we would be more at home in a Reform Synagogue, as it was similar to the services that were held at Norwood.

We chose to become members of the West London Synagogue at Upper Berkeley Street. We attended service regularly on Shabbos morning and admired the mixed choir and the wonderful organ, and decided we liked the service very much. Many years later, when we lived in Golders Green and we joined Alyth Gardens, nearer to our home, my cousin Harold would buy me a special ticket so that I could attend the Yom Kippur service at Upper Berkeley Street, at that time presided over by Rabbi Hugo Gryn.

On Friday nights, our family would gather for the Shabbos dinner. I remember how Harold would bury himself behind the latest copies of the *Jewish Chronicle*, much to Auntie Esther's indignation.

News about my Teacher's Exchange

After Hans had left for South Africa, I had applied for an opportunity to work as a teacher on exchange, so I could join him.

Years went by and I heard nothing. I still saw all my school friends. I still went out with Harry M and Albert L. I even acquired a new boyfriend, and we often enjoyed many a meal together; but all the time I wrote every week regularly to Hans. He would reply probably once a fortnight. My writing is large because I am short-sighted, and I had a rather peculiar print learnt at my school, which made us do some sort of italic writing. I easily filled the five pages, which was the maximum allowed to be sent by air.

Hans, on the contrary, wrote in a small, beautiful, cursive writing and got at least double the amount into the five pages. From his letters I saw that he was still working at this rather boring job with the CTC Bazaars. He seemed to be constantly changing the place where he lived. I used to have some of his letters, but I put them in such a safe place that today I don't know where they are!

In September 1937, a letter came from the Teacher's Exchange System with the information that a teaching post had been reserved for me

Chapter Fourteen. Letters from South Africa. Sad News

to start the following January in Pretoria, Transvaal, South Africa. I was to exchange jobs with a teacher from South Africa for one year. They urged me to book my passage without delay. Without a second thought, I took myself off to the Union Castle Line offices and booked a return ticket in the tourist class. I chose quite a nice cabin with a porthole, which I was to share with two other women. The journey would take two weeks.

My mother and family were very good in that they did not put any obstacle in my way. My mother immediately began looking out for suitable dresses and also a cabin trunk which opened like a wardrobe and was steel-lined. One side was for shelves and the other for hanging space. You could never ever move it yourself. It was so heavy that I needed a porter to move it. It was to go into the hold and I had another suitcase to provide for me in the cabin itself. My journey was to start the day before Christmas 1937.

The staff at Addison Gardens gave me a farewell lunch. When I told Harry I was going to South Africa, he asked me if it was because of the man I had met at the dance some time before, and I had to admit it was true. Young Levine told me, long after, that he couldn't believe that I was suddenly going to the end of the world; but I was excited and full of anticipation.

I wrote to Hans to tell him my news, and at that very moment the CTC Bazaars offered him a good job in Port Elizabeth, miles and miles away from Johannesburg and Pretoria. He refused the job because he knew I was coming, and then they gave him the sack.

He began working as a commercial traveller. This was quite a usual occupation for young men. He would borrow Willie Schapiro's little Opel car, fill it with clothes and dresses and drive into the country to the remote little villages (dorps). There would be a general store, which was very often run by a Jewish owner, and more and more by an Afrikaner. All of these remote shops were quite willing to buy from his stock.

He made friends with someone called Rudi Hirsch, who imported goods from Palestine. It was called Palestine Industries and sold many things coming from what is now Israel. Hans was very enterprising and successful.

The time came for me to leave London. My mother came with me to Southampton. Before long I was on the boat, waving goodbye to her. It was only then that I realised that there was my poor mother in the same position as I had been when Hans had left. I realised then how she must have felt saying goodbye to her only daughter, be it only for a year. I promised myself that I would write to her every week, which I did most faithfully for many years. When I went down to my cabin, there was a little bouquet of heather wishing me luck and lots of love from Auntie Esther.

Chapter Fifteen.

I LEAVE FOR SOUTH AFRICA

I shall never forget my voyage to South Africa on the *Dunnotar Castle*, one of the ships of the Union Castle line. I did not stay for long on the deck but went down to my cabin to unpack. The next morning, I awoke with a headache and a terrible feeling of nausea.

Christmas Day, and I have a vague memory of people going in for the special Christmas dinner as I lay prostrate on my berth, hardly able to turn my head from left to right. I thought to myself, 'Why did I ever come on this trip? I will never be able to return to England!' But, as we left the Bay of Biscay and the sea calmed down, I gradually recovered from my bout of sea-sickness.

Soon after that, we arrived at Madeira, a beautiful island off the coast of Portugal. The ship was too big to enter the port, so we were taken on little boats to the land. I noticed groups of people on the shore looking at us with serious and unsmiling faces. This against a backdrop of this picturesque island, a blaze of bright colour and sunlight. Many people spent their time buying hand-embroidered tablecloths, children's dresses, wine and different kinds of basketry. I wanted to look everywhere, because it was so different to anything that I had seen before.

I remember we went up to the top of the island by ox wagon and then slid down all the way on a sort of sledge, which was great fun, waving to everybody as if we were the king and queen. It was evening when we returned to the ship.

Another wonderful sight was when we sailed past Las Palmas, capital of Gran Canaria, a cone-shaped volcanic island, and saw a glorious sunset behind us to the west. After that, there was no sign of land for a long time, and for the rest of the journey we saw only the sea. We passed a sister ship on its homeward-bound trip to England with all the lights lit up, and there was much hooting of horns between the two ships.

By now I had met all the teachers who were also going on this exchange programme to South Africa. There were eight of us, single women from all parts of England. They were older than me and seemed to have more experience of travelling. Some had been on an exchange to Canada. We became close friends and generally we kept to ourselves. Every morning at about eleven o'clock, we sat on the deck and enjoyed the best food of the day – a cup of beef tea. The quality of the food deteriorated as the journey progressed.

When we were about to arrive in Cape Town, I was up, ready and dressed before the others were on deck. They seemed to still be moving about in their cabins. I was the only one on deck looking towards the land. What an amazing sight, approaching Cape Town harbour and seeing the majestic grandeur of Table Mountain rising up from the sea! It was like the backdrop in a theatre. Words cannot capture the sense of the drama I felt at the sight of such beauty: this enormous flat-topped mountain, Table Mountain, against a clear sky; for, on this occasion, there were no clouds floating on the summit – in other words, no tablecloth.

The ship docked very early in the morning and I looked down on an empty quayside, where I could just about discern only one man who was standing alone. I was expecting to meet an old friend of

Chapter Fifteen. I leave for South Africa

my mother. I looked down and guessed that the person I saw must be Mr Isaac Goodman, who had come to meet me. I called down, 'Mr Goodman?' and he answered, 'Miss Pearson?'; and he told me to come to the departure office on the boat, where he would meet me.

When I arrived at the office, he got me through Customs almost immediately. I don't know what happened to my trunk. He must have sent it to the railway station. I only had my suitcase to carry as we went down the gangway together. We walked to a large black motor-car, where his wife was sitting in the front passenger seat, awaiting my arrival. I didn't realise at the time how fortunate I was to be met in this way and shown such warmth and hospitality. I think they were just as excited as I was, meeting the daughter of old friends from Liverpool.

After all these years, the couple still spoke with strong Liverpudlian accents. I knew from my mother that Isaac Goodman was the secretary of the Jewish Board of Deputies, an important position in the Jewish community.

Mrs Goodman's mother had lived in Liverpool and had kept a boarding house for actors and actresses. My mother said Mrs Goodman told the story of how one night one of the guests who came to stay in their boarding house had a bear that slept at the foot of his bed.

I knew the Goodmans' son quite well. He came to our Seder at Norwood every year. He was a lawyer and one of his responsibilities was working for the *Daily Mirror*. My mother spoke to him about her case, hoping he would be able to help her to get a divorce. But this was never successful.

The Goodmans made me most welcome. They lived in a flat in Sea Point, a nearby suburb of Cape Town, and had prepared a lovely meal for me. Much of our conversations were spent enquiring about my family. Long ago they had all been to school together at The Liverpool Hebrew School. Mr Goodman gave me addresses of his relations in Johannesburg and handed me letters of introduction.

Mrs Goodman said to me, 'Why do you want to go to Johannesburg? Stay here with us. There are a lot of nice Jewish boys in Cape Town.' But I was eager to take the train to see Hans.

The Train Journey

When I arrived at the train station, my friends from the boat had saved me a place in their compartment. This train went all the way from Cape Town to Johannesburg and took two nights and nearly two days (c1000 miles). A compartment consisted of two long seats, two people on each side, four to a compartment. There were windows looking out and a small table between the two window seats. On the other side was the window looking onto the corridor. We gazed in admiration at the mountain ranges and the beautiful countryside until it was time for dinner.

We walked along the corridor to the restaurant. All four of us sat together at a table. When it was time to return to our compartment, night had fallen and our compartment had been transformed. The two long seats were converted into four sleeping berths with blankets, sheets and pillows. The table was now a wash basin and mirror. There were Venetian-type blinds at all the windows, and so we undressed and tucked ourselves into these beds and the rocking train soon sent us off to sleep.

When we woke in the morning, I peered through the blinds and saw a very different scene: hot blinding sun and the vast openness of the Karoo Desert. I prayed that Johannesburg would look different.

Chapter Fifteen. I leave for South Africa

In later years, I realised this semi-desert landscape has a special charm of its own.

We were on a steam train and occasional stops were made. I remember stopping at the town called Kimberley, where a male friend of one of my companions came to the window and said, 'Don't have anything to do with Afrikaans men.' I hadn't the faintest intention of having anything to do with Afrikaans men – I'm not sure I even knew who they were!

The service was extremely good on the train and we had all our meals in the restaurant. A man of mixed race, dressed in a linen uniform, looked after us and could not have been more helpful. He converted the compartments from day to night and from night to day. The time soon passed and after the second night I knew that we were approaching Johannesburg. My friends were all very excited for me and I took special care to look my best. The train steamed into Johannesburg and there, almost opposite our carriage, stood Hans with a bunch of rather forlorn-looking marigolds, but he looked just the same as I had remembered. It was wonderful to see him.

There he stood before me – tall, broad and handsome as ever and so very familiar. I forgot all about my travelling companions. I don't know what happened to them. All I remember was stepping off the train and being locked in a tight hug with Hans.

What happened exactly I can't quite remember, as I was so excited. We must have put my trunk in the left luggage office and then, as we stepped out of the station, Hans brought me to where a little German Opel car was parked. He had borrowed the car from his friend Willy Shapiro. He then drove me around Johannesburg. All I remember seeing of Johannesburg were the big, tall, hill-shaped mine dumps that must have been taken out of the goldmines. Johannesburg was not very prepossessing.

A New Life Begins

Eventually, Hans drove me out to Germiston, an outlying suburb, 'along the reef' (the gold reef), where Willy Schapiro lived with his wife and daughter. They had opened a dress shop, and in a short time it had done very well. They gave us a very tasty dinner, and afterwards Willy, his wife and Hans sat at a piano, singing a song from a sheet of music they had just bought. It was George Formby singing *Little Lady Comes By*. I suddenly felt very tired and was much quieter than my usual self. This was not only because of the long journey behind me, but because Johannesburg is very high up and everyone feels breathless when they first arrive.

The next day, Hans drove me to Pretoria, where I was going to teach. It was about an hour's drive from Johannesburg. Halfway through the journey, Hans said, 'Would you like to see where General Smuts lives?' General Smuts was very well known to the English population and I was interested to see his home and the village called Irene. We didn't see his home, but we went to the small village store run by a Mr Cohen. He welcomed us and quickly introduced me to two relations of his from Pretoria. The first was Ann Cohen, who was his daughter-in-law, and the second was Sarah Zway, who may have been a relation of his, but I'm not sure. When they heard I was going to teach in Pretoria, they were extremely interested. Ann gave me her address and telephone number and said I must ring her when I was settled.

We left and drove on to Pretoria. We arrived at Church Square, and there in the centre stood a large statue of Paul Kruger. First, I went into the Pretoria Town Hall offices to meet Mr Cullingworth, the person in charge of arrangements for exchange teachers. He gave me directions how to reach the school in a place called Wonderboom, where I was to teach, and also handed me a list of suitable boarding houses.

Chapter Fifteen. I leave for South Africa

Hans and I then drove towards the Union Buildings. Pretoria appeared an attractive town, the roads lined with fragrant-smelling, flowering jacaranda trees. The attractive Union Buildings were the seat of the administrative capital of South Africa and stood high on a hill, a dramatic sight, with green lawns sloping down to the street. These buildings were designed by Sir Herbert Baker, an architect responsible for major buildings throughout the British Empire. He designed South Africa House that stands in Trafalgar Square in London. The buildings he designed can also be seen in India.

The first place I visited was a boarding house called Lockley's. I was shown into a pleasant room: comfortable, quite roomy and facing this wonderful view of the Union Buildings. It was fifteen pounds a month, which included all meals. If you were out for lunch, they provided you with sandwiches. Fifteen pounds was my monthly salary from England. I had additional money and I couldn't resist this charming room. I found afterwards my exchange friends were living close by. I left my suitcase in the room and Hans and I explored the grounds of the Union Buildings. Then we went to see the town of Wonderboom and have a look at the school where I was to teach; but, of course, as it was the weekend it was closed.

We found where I was to catch the bus in Beatrix Street, not far from Lockley's Boarding House. At my first meal, the people in Lockley's were warm and friendly. Some of the food was quite strange to me. I had never, for instance, seen sweetcorn, which they called a mealie. 'However do you eat this?' I said to my neighbour.

'You take it in your hands,' he replied. 'Go on,' he said, much to everyone's laughter. It was the same with avocado pear, which I had never tasted or seen before.

Eventually, Hans had to return to Germiston, and for the first time I went back to my new room, unpacked and settled down for the night.

Teaching in South Africa

The next day I took the bus from Beatrix Street to the school. I went into the headmaster's office and introduced myself. There was no welcome or smile. He just stood up and said, 'I will take you to your class. Here is the register. We have prayers in a quarter of an hour.' And that was that. The children in my class were five to six years old and were all white. I was left to introduce myself to them, and I told them I had just come off a boat from a far-away country called England. They looked at me with great interest and were far friendlier than their headmaster.

I then opened the register. Now that represented a difficulty, as I couldn't pronounce some of the names. For instance, I pronounced Labuscharn as if it were French, whereas it had to be pronounced as a Dutchman would pronounce it: with a guttural *c*. The children giggled quietly behind their hands, but I managed to carry on.

When we returned from prayers, I simply had to go by the timetable and do my best. The children helped me by showing me their text books and exercise books. When it came to playtime, two very friendly teachers from Scotland came in to welcome me and took me up to the staff room, where I ate my packed sandwiches. They said that there was a male teacher who would give us a lift there and back from Beatrix Street every day. All that I had to do was make a contribution towards the petrol.

I told them that I wasn't used to teaching class-based mathematics, but rather helping each child individually. I would rather teach in a way that allows for the child to work at their own level. Since that first day, I had never spoken to the headmaster, but one day I found him sitting next to the piano in the hall with a notebook in his hand, ready to observe how I took the class for Music and Movement, as if he were a school inspector. I really didn't mind, and I took the

Chapter Fifteen. I leave for South Africa

lesson as usual, playing the piano, singing, acting out songs and encouraging the children to listen to the various rhythms that I played. The children responded well.

We then lined up to go back to our classroom; still not a word from the headmaster. This didn't worry me in the slightest. First of all, I had taken Music as a special subject at college. Also, I had learned a great deal from my very musical Aunt Annie. I knew that I had taken a good lesson. School ended at three o'clock every day.

I considered the hours of work easy, despite finding the methods of teaching rather dull. I remember on one occasion how, when it started to rain, and the children were going home, they took off their shoes, carried them and ran home in bare feet – the last thing children would do in England.

I will never forget an occasion when a male teacher gave me and two Scottish teachers a lift in his car. I saw a lorry, with many African men in striped jerseys jammed in together. 'Look at all those men, packed in,' I exclaimed. I had never seen so many men crowded into one lorry.

'They are not men,' he said. 'They are kaffirs.'

I was aware there was racial discrimination in South Africa, but here was something else – a way of thinking that a black person was not a human being. This shocked me. I was silent. My two friends sitting at the back of the car told me afterwards how embarrassed they felt by his comment.

While I was still at the school, this man left the teaching profession and went to supervise African men working on the roads.

New Friends

Meanwhile, I had a very interesting social life. I soon found out my two friends, who were also on exchange teaching, were living in the same road and not far away. After a day or two, I rang up the lady that I had met at Irene's named Mrs Ann Cohen and she immediately invited me to dinner. She collected me the same day and took me to her large, pleasant house. I was introduced to her husband and their three little children. She was extremely friendly and not long afterwards her friend, Mrs Sarah Zway, also invited me to her home.

I remember she lived at 8 Myrtle Street, and her mother and sister lived opposite. Sarah and her husband Norman made me most welcome. The Zways had a daughter Hilda and a son called Stanley. This young boy had suffered from polio and as a result his legs were encased in iron supports. I was welcome to go there whenever I chose and on each occasion was asked to join them for a meal.

In London we ate plain English food, but when I visited the Zways' home I tasted for the first time eastern European Jewish cuisine, such as delicious borscht. Sarah had been born in Palestine, but Norman had come from a Polish village. They first had a business in the Northern Transvaal, but now, being more affluent, had moved to Pretoria, where Norman owned a large Garden Nursery. Every week in Pretoria I seemed to meet other members of the Jewish community and everyone made me most welcome and went out of their way to make me feel very much at home. Perhaps it was unusual at that time to entertain someone from overseas?

Hans came to see me every Wednesday and we met at the weekends, either in Pretoria or Johannesburg. I met his friends, many of whom were refugees from Germany. Meanwhile, Mr Cullingworth, who was in charge of the whole exchange system in Pretoria, had arranged some visits to educational institutions, which he thought would be of interest to us. I missed most of those because they were usually at weekends. He asked my friends, 'Where is Miss Pearson? Is she too shy to join us?' And they said, 'No. She has a boyfriend in Johannesburg.' This seemed to please him.

Eventually, we did meet. He took us first to a girls school run by a headmistress who was the sister of Vera Brittain. The second visit was to a small purpose-built nursery school introduced by a Canadian, Dr Ruth Arndt.

Meanwhile, Hans and I made plans for the future. Hans was still working successfully as a commercial traveller, but I don't think he was happy in his work. I said to him, 'Why don't you become a teacher? It's very easy.' I had no knowledge of the pay. I was rather unworldly in this respect.

He said, 'What a good idea.'

Once his doctorate from Germany was recognised, he would only need one year's training at The Normal College in Johannesburg. After he had finished his training, we hoped to get married in London.

My term at Pretoria ended and I moved to Johannesburg, where I was employed to spend the next two terms of my exchange year.

Travelling in South Africa

In the holidays I went with Hans on one of his business trips to the Orange Free State. What an experience! Vast landscapes, long and empty roads covering vast distances. We would stop at small villages, called 'dorps' in Afrikaans, where there would be one general store, very often run by a Jewish couple. Here Hans would sell his goods. Apparently, these general stores were increasingly being taken over by the Afrikaners. On this journey we came across a group of African women, naked to the waist, in their tribal dress. They smiled and appeared friendly and Hans took a photograph of me standing with them.

We travelled into Basutoland, which was an English protectorate. We met a Basuto man riding one of their famous ponies. Hans asked if he could go for a ride on his pony. The next thing, Hans is galloping off into the distance and out of sight. I thought to myself: here I am by myself in South Africa. Hans has ridden off and left me here all alone; but, of course, he returned.

In Johannesburg, I found new accommodation in a hotel called St Bees. I have no recollection of the school where I worked. I had a number of letters of introduction both from the family in London and the Goodmans in Cape Town. I contacted and met Mr Goodman's widowed sister-in-law and her daughter Phyllis. They welcomed me into their home. Phyllis' brother Edward worked in one of these village general stores called Ottostaal, and we visited him. I was invited out a great deal. One young man, who had recently returned from Oxford, asked me to marry him. And in that way the year went by.

In the school holiday I went with two other women to the Game Reserve, which is in the Northern Transvaal. That was an experience. The trip was organised by a woman who was a refugee from Germany. She did the driving. On the way there we spent two nights in our tent, which we pitched before we slept.

She was inexperienced at driving over the corrugated South African roads. You had to go over them quickly, but she bumped over them slowly. We stayed one night in a tent in a town park and in the early morning we were awoken by the sound of animals munching grass. It was a relief to know that they were only cows.

When we first arrived in the Game Reserve we stayed for one night at each of the big campsites. One was called Skucuza. After that night we went up to the northern part of the Game Reserve and stayed in a smaller and most beautiful campsite called Shingoetsi. We would wake up early in the morning, when it was just beginning to get light, and go out into the forest, where you would perhaps see vultures eating the remains of a kill. You might see a family of lions walking alongside the cars or a group resting under the trees. We saw herds of impala and zebra and occasionally a giraffe. The authorities warned us that if we met a female elephant we should make a hasty retreat. Personally, I wouldn't have been able to tell the sex of an elephant so easily, so if we saw an elephant we certainly did beat a hasty retreat!

One early evening, the car got stuck in the mud and we couldn't move. We were very nervous, but the authorities in the small campsite realised we had not returned and found us. They pulled us out, much to our relief. When I came back from this holiday, Hans said I seemed to be a bit of a nervous wreck.

Chapter Sixteen.

MY DECISION TO REMAIN

At the end of the year, Hans hired a house in Johannesburg from one of his friends, where we could stay in comfort. Hans and myself and somebody called Fish went to live there for four weeks, whilst the owners were away. And, most remarkable of all, my headmistress from Addison Gardens, London, Mrs Bottrill, came out for the holiday, as she had just retired. She stayed in the house with us. She had always been a friendly and jolly person and a very good headmistress.

My exchange year had come to an end and I decided not to go back to England but to stay for another year. It was 1938. I obtained leave of absence, without pay, from London County Council and looked in the newspapers for a teaching post, bearing in mind I was not allowed to teach in a Government school as I did not speak Afrikaans. Almost immediately I saw a post advertised in Pretoria. It was to run a nursery school. I sent in my application and was invited to meet the chairman. This was the Canadian Dr Ruth Arndt. They had already opened two schools in the West End of Pretoria and had invited Margaret Tasman from London to come out and be in charge of both schools.

Margaret and I soon became firm friends and remained so for the rest of our lives. We were both equally qualified. Margaret told me that there had previously been a Miss Pearson employed at the West

Chapter Sixteen. My Decision to Remain

End school and Dr Arndt's husband couldn't get over the fact that he once found her scrubbing the floor. Apparently, this, for a South African, was considered most unusual. The fact that I had the same name of Pearson was very much in my favour. At this time there were no trained nursery school teachers in South Africa. I am sure that they were pleased to employ me, and so I returned to Pretoria.

This happened at the beginning of January 1938. I rented a room near where I had lived before. There were no cooking facilities. I had lunch at the school and in the evening I usually dined with friends; or, if not, Margaret and I managed something together. Margaret lived quite near me. Her name was Margaret Tasman, but we called her Tas. Our pay was very small.

The school was small and purpose-built. It provided education for white people of limited means, often labelled in South Africa as 'poor whites'. The small bungalows surrounding the school were in a poor condition. I noticed that the cars parked outside were nearly bigger than the houses. The children, provided they were not ill, would come at about 9 o'clock. They would stay all morning, have a hot lunch in school, followed by an afternoon rest. They slept on little canvas folding beds. The day ended with the singing of a song or listening to a story. In some ways I felt very frustrated because although the children spoke some English, it was obvious that they were more fluent in Afrikaans. Tas used to come to me two or three days a week, sharing her time between the two nursery schools. I had no other help, except for a tall caretaker, who was someone of mixed race.

There were about twenty-five to thirty children. I remember one incident when all the children were asleep on their little beds and I noticed a most peculiar creature, about two and a half inches long, gripping the wall. It turned around and looked at me. Believe it or not, I walked straight out of the room, leaving the children lying asleep. I found the caretaker, who looked surprised at my dismay. It turned out to be a chameleon. He couldn't understand why I was so shocked and that I had never seen one before. And soon my first year at the Pretoria Nursery came to an end.

New Opportunities

I was gradually learning more about the Nursery School Movement and acquiring a greater knowledge of Infant Welfare. At that time there was a short training course at The Afrikaans University of Pretoria, and another in Johannesburg, with a nursery school run by Marjory Saunders from England, and a new training course was starting in Cape Town.

I learnt of a society called the Nursery School Association of South Africa that met from time to time. Dr Ruth Arndt was the Chairman. I attended meetings where she delivered some outstanding and inspiring talks. And this is how, by chance, I became closely involved in the Nursery School Movement, and this continued for the rest of my working life.

Dr Arndt gathered around her a group of important people living in Pretoria, and together they took responsibility for the organisation of the nursery schools in this city. Pretoria is the administrative capital of South Africa, and this meant that Dr Arndt had a wide choice of suitable members for her committee. My friend Tas had left her post and was now in charge of a more prestigious nursery school that I had once visited.

I was now in charge of a nursery school in the West End. The children here were all white, spoke English and came from more financially well-off homes. The school was in a very ordinary-looking small house while the new school was being built nearby. I was sent to visit a school in Johannesburg to get ideas for designs for the furniture.

Chapter Sixteen. My Decision to Remain

I remember two interesting events. The first was when I was asked to find a cook who would make the midday meal. My friends, the Goodmans, had recently moved to Pretoria and I asked Mrs Goodman if she would like to come and make the meal for the children each school day. She was delighted. I still remember her pleasure when she arrived with food and cooked them delicious meals. She loved cooking and derived great pleasure from cooking for little children. At the same time, she was pleased to earn some money.

I came into contact with Mr Middleton, a distinguished member of the committee. He was a retired civil servant. In fact, he had been the Chief Secretary of the South African Treasury. He came to see how I was keeping my accounts, which, of course, only involved a small amount of money. I hadn't the faintest idea how to keep accounts, especially up to his standards. He showed me how to keep and number the receipts for my petty cash. I was very fond of him and I loved to hear his strong Scottish accent. Not many people got the opportunity to be taught by such a distinguished person.

Through Dr Arndt, I made new friends. Nora McCullough from Canada and her American friend had started what they called an Arts Centre in Pretoria and Cape Town. Here, white children could come and paint and draw, enjoy books and toys. Nora and her friend were both very interesting people. I met Vera Webber, who was in charge of teaching young people about Child Welfare. She inspected the nursery schools to see that they were kept up to standard. I again met Mr Cullingworth and his family socially. The teacher with whom I had the exchange had now returned from England to South Africa. His name was Mr Brink, and I met with him, his wife and his mother.

I used to go to the cinema, if only to watch the Gaumont British News. There was no television and I didn't even own a radio. There was, of course, a daily newspaper, with fearful news coming out about Germany. In this year Hitler's increasing power was causing Europe great anxiety. I remember when he marched into Czechoslovakia. Hans was distressed and said that this would give Hitler access to the factories which were busy manufacturing weapons of war. We little knew at the time how this invasion affected the lives of countless Jews in Czechoslovakia.

Chapter 17.

OUR WEDDING

In January 1939, Hans started a year's course in Johannesburg at what was called The Normal College, and he was very busy with his studies. Whenever he had free time, he worked so as to earn money. I know that he went to some of the smaller villages (dorps) in the Transvaal, where he thought there might be some Jewish people, and talked to them about the work of The Jewish Board of Deputies. This was a good time for me. I recall feeling quite guilty that I never felt homesick.

During this year, Marcus's great friend Jack Rich came from London to Johannesburg to be in charge of the Johannesburg Board of Deputies. My mother must have prevailed on him to bring out my little Singer sewing machine, together with material and a pattern for me to make. I enjoyed making this warm and attractive new dress. I often stayed with Jack or with Hans's friend Nussbaum (whom we called *Nut Tree*), who was a photographer and had a studio, where I could stay over at weekends.

Meanwhile, the world situation was becoming increasingly dangerous as Hitler grew more powerful. When Chamberlain came back from his meeting with Hitler to declare that there would be peace in our time, many people were relieved, but Hans knew better and felt increasingly apprehensive. Nevertheless, we were planning to come to England at the end of the year so that the family could enjoy our wedding.

At the end of August 1939, Hans applied for a South African passport. His years in England and South Africa had made him eligible. His German passport was out of date and there was no hope of this ever being renewed. When war was declared in September, Hans had obtained his new passport just one week earlier. What a stroke of luck, for, if he had not received it, he would have been accounted as an enemy alien. Actually, this would not have been as serious for Hans as it was for Jewish refugees in Great Britain, but it would have been a handicap.

This meant that our planned trip to England and the proposed wedding was out of the question. I was very sad, and so were my family at home. I went straight out and bought quite an expensive radio, as it was so vital to hear the news.

When my friend Sarah Zway heard of our disappointment, right away she said, 'Well, I'll make the wedding. You can be married from our house.' We arranged for the wedding to take place at the end of the school year, which happened to be 10th December and the fifth day of Chanukah. Sarah arranged it all. We visited Rabbi Hirsch and then Sarah and her husband Norman arranged everything, including how it should be choral and floral in the shul, and nobody was going to charge us a penny. I went out alone to a shop called Foschini's and bought a blue linen dress and jacket to match for £3.50, which was very reasonable and just what I wanted. My mother sent me a blue handbag and gloves. I bought my shoes and hat locally.

WE GET MARRIED

I woke very early on my wedding day feeling unwell, and I phoned Sarah. I said: 'I don't think I can be married today.'

Chapter 17. Our Wedding

She came around immediately, took me in her car to her home and tucked me into her own bed. She called the doctor, who gave me a sedative and I fell asleep. She said, 'Don't worry about all your belongings in your room. I'll pack and collect them for you.' The day went by and I began to feel better. By the time I was due to get dressed, I was my old self again, much to my surprise.

We had already arranged to have a colour film taken of the wedding. This was a new invention in South Africa. We have the short five-minute, very colourful film to this day. The reason we went to all this expense was because I wanted to send it home to my family in London so that they could at least watch the wedding. The film cost £5 to make. I knew that my family had held a little celebration in London and had invited a few friends to join them. Norman Zway gave me away and Sarah walked behind. She had produced a beautiful corsage of fresh flowers, which made my dress look very attractive. I remember she said to me, 'Don't smile at anyone when you go in. Keep your eyes down'; and this I did.

I had invited many of my friends. Amongst them was Dr Lowenthal, who had originally come from Germany to Liverpool, who had brought me into the world and was highly thought of by all the family. On his retirement, he had come to live in Johannesburg with his son. He came from Johannesburg, as did Marcus's friend Jack Rich. I have already mentioned Jack had recently come to South Africa to become the Secretary of the Jewish Board of Deputies in Johannesburg.

The shul was decorated. There were flowers draped around the chuppah. The choir sang and there was Hans waiting for me with Nussbaum as his best man. After the ceremony, we all returned to Sarah's home at No 8 Myrtle Street. She had arranged three large tables in her dining room with a lovely tea. We welcomed all the guests as they came in. I remember that Hans gave a speech. But at that stage I was rather tongue-tied. As the early evening approached, Sarah and Norman took us down to the station and we boarded the famous train that would take us all the way to Cape Town. I remember how she ran after the train, waving goodbye to us.

Hans had said to me that we could either have a honeymoon or an engagement ring. We couldn't afford both. I chose the honeymoon.

When we arrived in Cape Town, we spent the first two weeks on a farm in Somerset West. It was close to the sea and there were horses you could ride. After the second week, Hans's friend Authur Graetzer, who was now working in Cape Town, found us a good hotel close to the sea in Camps Bay. I remember we were able to see the Goodmans. The time passed quickly and after the four weeks we returned to Pretoria.

Hans had been appointed to a teaching post in the famous gymnasium where Churchill had been imprisoned during the Boer War. I returned to my nursery school in the West End. After the first term, we found a flat to rent quite near to the Union Buildings. We had a bedroom, a sitting room, a small kitchen, a bathroom and a lovely veranda (which we called a stoep).

It's a strange thing in South Africa, but, as far as I could see, no Jewish people ever bought anything retail. We bought a few pieces of secondhand furniture and three reasonably priced new chairs. There was some discussion over a carpet. Hans wanted a cheaper one. I called in Vera Webber and she agreed with me, much to Hans's surprise. This was a very happy time. I recall we used to divide our money carefully: some for food, some for rent and some for personal pleasures. Money for personal pleasures never quite lasted to the end of the month, but we managed somehow.

Tallman & Philcox (school-friends) standing next to Marcus, pilots with the Royal Flying Corps, First World War, France circ. 1916.

Germany 1918, Front right, my cousin, Marcus, aged 19 (Prisoner of war.)

Wing Commander Marcus Kaye, Second World War.

Captain Hans Freund (known in the Army as Harold Friend) with the S.A. 5th Brigade.

Hans began work in the army as an aerial photographer.

Information Officers with the S.A. 5th Brigade ;
Leo Marquard, John Quarrie, Reg Webber. Hans, Oppermann.

Chapter Eighteen.

WAR IS DECLARED

The war had begun, although it seemed, where we lived, as if nothing much was happening. Hans, with Norman and a few other friends, had volunteered to keep guard on certain important sites. South Africa had joined the war, but there were many Afrikaners who still had bitter memories of the Boer War and their sympathies lay with Germany. They were more concerned with taking power in South Africa from the British than fighting the Second World War.

On thinking about these times and now having a greater knowledge of the South African scene, it seems surprising that I was not more affected by the fact that the African people in South Africa had no voice in the governing of the country. There was this division made between who was black and who was white. Was it because I had very little contact with the great majority of black people living in the country that I was not more aware of it all? My social circle was restricted.

It was then that my lack of knowledge of cooking was revealed. I had never lived in an ordinary home, and wherever I had lived there had always been a professional cook. I remember scrambling an egg with a large Mrs Beeton cook book in front of me. Hans was much amused and took a photograph. My mother had sent out two large wooden boxes containing linen and two sets of china: one for best and one for every day. I've got the one called Floradora to this very day. This was my best set. My mother wrote that she and Auntie Annie had gone down to the docks to place the boxes in the hold. I kept those boxes for many a year.

I introduced Hans to all my friends. He had an attractive and strong personality and people took to him very easily. We made new friends during these happy times. It was only later that I discovered that Hans had a very strong, deep bass baritone voice. Perhaps he didn't realise it himself.

However, early in 1940, Germany broke through the Maginot Line from their fortresses along the Siegfried Line and the whole situation became more fraught. Poland, France and even North Africa were invaded. As a result, Hans decided that it was his duty to join forces against the power of Hitler. We discussed it and we both agreed this was the right thing to do. The South African forces were entirely voluntary. There was no conscription.

There was a large Army training camp outside Pretoria. Hans went there to volunteer. He joined the photographic section, and this meant he had to fly an aeroplane and learn to take aerial photographs. He joined as a Private and was soon wearing khaki shorts and tunic. Although he was stationed at the camp, he was still able to come home most nights. I remember Mr Middleton wanted to invite us to go to the dance at his golf club. He told us that they would not allow him to invite us because Hans was not an officer.

Old Middleton was furious and said that if they did not allow it he would resign. After that they permitted us to be invited and we went dancing together among the officers. I don't think Hans enjoyed doing this photography, and he told me he was as sick as anything when the aeroplane swerved; but he said he hoped he would get used to it. He had been given leave of absence from his school.

Chapter Eighteen. War is Declared

One of Dr Arndt's friends, E. G. Malherbe, had been asked by the Army to form a new unit. It was for Information Officers. Their duty would be to keep soldiers aware of the news and ongoing developments and, importantly, why we were at war. This involved explaining about Germany, Hitler and the rise of the Nazi party. The officer to be in charge of this new unit was to be this very doctor, E. G. Malherbe. I had previously met him, and I knew that he had been commissioned to devise Intelligence Tests suitable for the South African public. Much to my surprise, he had invited me to take part in this experiment. I had to ask the questions that he had devised. I suppose he thought that, coming from another country, I would be more objective.

Hans was chosen to be an information officer with the rank of Second Lieutenant. His knowledge of German, Afrikaans and English was a decided advantage. I met a number of members of his team, all of whom were white. A few had come from Fort Hare, including Alan Slee, originally from England, and his wife Elaine. Fort Hare was a well-known institution giving further education to Africans.

The officer with whom Hans would have most contact was a fine Afrikaner called Leo Marquard, who I think came from Natal. Hans had a very high respect for Leo – I think it was mutual.

Hans looked quite grand in his new uniform, with all its badges and military tokens on the lapels. Very soon the company were informed that they would be joining the Fifth South African Brigade and would be leaving South Africa for the war zone in North Africa. They would be going up to Cairo by boat, through the Suez Canal. At last the fact that he would be leaving dawned on me and I thought that perhaps it would be a good idea to try for a baby before he left.

AS TIME GOES BY

Hans leaves for North Africa

A week or two later, when Hans was due to leave, I knew that I was pregnant. Soon, I was standing on the platform of Pretoria station. The train was packed with soldiers of the Fifth Brigade. Hans's last words to me were: 'How are you going to manage?' and I said with my usual ignorance and over-confidence: 'I shall be quite all right.'

The train left, and I returned to my little flat. It seemed very empty and I felt very alone. One of the wives – Elaine Slee – had agreed to come and stay with me, and this would be a comfort. It was several days before she arrived, and they were the loneliest days I had ever experienced. I was still teaching at a school in the West End. During the last weekend that Hans and I spent together, the Nursery School was due to be moved into its new buildings. The Nursery School Committee was very sympathetic and moved the school equipment for me. After that, it was a pleasure to be in this new, fresh and suitably designed little Nursery School.

I had started having morning sickness and a terrible craving for apricots of every kind: fresh, stewed, tinned. Gradually, the nausea left me. Sarah Zway suggested that I would be better off staying at a Boarding House that was close by and run by two elderly Jewish women from London. I sub-let the flat and moved into Surrey Lodge. Here I had good company and regular, tasty food. While I was there I made a few new friends, including Bruno Raikin, a well-known pianist. I already knew his sister and his relations, the Neumanns. Some of these friends, like the Neumanns, are on my wedding film. When I was five months pregnant, I gave in my notice as I thought it was time I took things more easily.

I now started preparing for the arrival of the baby. Vera Webber – who was in charge of teaching Nursery Nursing – came with me to buy whatever was necessary. I bought three dozen towelling

Chapter Eighteen. War is Declared

napkins and one dozen Harington squares, which were thinner. I think I bought little vests and material to make the first nightgowns the baby would wear. They were magyar in shape and open at the back, which made for easy changing of the nappy, with a little embroidery round the neck. The nappies would have to be washed by hand as there were no disposable ones in those days and I had no washing machine.

Only now did I let my family in London know that I was pregnant and soon to give birth. I had postponed this news as I did not want them to worry too much.

As far as I knew, there was no facility for maternity leave. Such concerns for women did not exist. I had recently heard from my friend Dink's sister, Lillian Craigie, who was living in Natal. Her husband was in the Royal Air Force and at the beginning of the North African Campaign all wives had been evacuated to Natal. She suggested I come to Natal for a holiday. I had known her well before her marriage. I went to the station and booked the holiday in Uvanga and prepared for the trip. I spent my last month's wages on the fare.

That very night, as I lay in bed, I awoke and was aware that somebody had climbed through my window, which I had stupidly left open. They were shining a torch into the chest of drawers. My heart was beating. I was so terrified and could not open my mouth to scream for help. The burglar must have heard me move and quickly disappeared out of the window. Only then was I able to raise the alarm. He had taken my handbag with all my tickets, but hardly any money, as it had all gone towards the holiday – the only loss was a pretty coral necklace that I had owned since childhood. I felt better after a day or two. The railway officials, however, gave me a new ticket when they heard the situation and I was able to make my plans. Sadly, my dear friend Lillian wrote to tell me that her husband had just been killed by the Free French Air Force (I think when the English were trying to destroy the French Navy. Germany had overrun France and the so-called Free French were unwilling to lose their Navy.)

Lillian was left with her young twins, a girl and a boy. She met me at Uvanga station and took me to the hotel where I had booked to stay. She was a very brave woman. The hotel was right by the sea – very beautiful – and the care I was given was a great treat. I spent the two weeks with her and the rest of the wives. They tried to persuade me to stay with them and said they would look after me, but I had already arranged to return to Pretoria.

Bad News

During the weeks that followed, I had one interesting experience which illustrated the famous song, '*Kol Yisrael Avorim*' (All Israel are brothers). Sarah Zway had invited me for tea. There was a new friend of hers that I had never met before – she had come from Upington in the Northern Transvaal, a very remote and isolated town. Her name was Mrs Helfet. When she saw me, she announced that my relations the Reeds were the best-dressed family in Liverpool. She had known the whole family and had come from Liverpool to South Africa to marry and had gone by ox wagon from Cape Town to Upington. It must have taken weeks, if not months. Incidentally, years later one of her sons had become an orthopaedic specialist in Cape Town, and when I needed advice he treated me and would never accept a penny.

During the following weeks, I received letters from Hans. In 1941, he had been in Cairo and had moved to a desert camp near to the sea. He was stationed at the South African 5th Brigade Headquarters. He sent me a photograph of himself, in the nude, standing with a friend – holding a pith helmet in front of a rather strategic place. He had a wicked sense of humour.

Chapter Eighteen. War is Declared

On 24th November, I awoke to hear the news that the 5th Brigade Headquarters had been surrounded two days earlier by Rommel's forces at the Battle of Sidi Rezegh, now in Libya. The news gave me a terrible shock. I spoke to my friends in Pretoria and in Johannesburg, who tried to console me over this frightening news, but the only one who gave me some comfort was Willie Hirsch, who said to me: 'You know, Kitty, if anyone can get out of this situation – it will be your Hans.'

I don't know the actual date when I was informed that he was alive but had been captured. Sarah Zway invited me to her house. I saw Rabbi Hirsch sitting there. It was the duty of the religious Ministers to inform the next of kin of any news. For one horrible moment, I thought: Is he going to tell me Hans is dead? – but he simply told me that he had been captured, which I already knew.

Some time later, I heard that Hans had escaped, had been wounded in the foot and was recovering in a hospital in Cairo. The news gradually filtered down to us, but I think it best to relate the actual details in Hans's own words as recorded in an official report that he submitted to the authorities. He was asked to produce this account. The report starts as Hans had returned from ten days' leave, which he had spent in Palestine, during which he had visited many friends and relations – such as Paul Freund and his cousin Ilse. They were surprised to see him dressed as a Captain in the South African Army and tried to persuade him – unsuccessfully – to give them his gun.

They had escaped from Germany and made their way to what was then Palestine, and their situation was insecure, and they would have valued the possession of a gun. When Hans returned to Cairo, he found that his Unit had gone forward into the desert and it took him some time to find where they were now stationed. Eventually, he succeeded and took part in the ensuing battle of Sidi Rezegh. It was following that action that he was captured, together with other men.

Very few survivors. My Cousin Marcus, with a box camera took this photo on the first day of liberation of Bergen-Belsen.

My cousin Marcus, although a very modest man had a distinguished career in the RAF. He was recalled as soon as the Second World War was declared and eventually was consigned to work with Field marshal Montgomery.

He took part in Dunkirk; Dieppe and he was one of the first in the liberation of Belsen. He accompanied the Jewish Chaplain and took photographs of what he saw. At the end of the war he was awarded the OBE for his services.

Notice Bergen-Belsen Camp.

Bergen-Belsen Camp Grave no 8.

Bergen-Belsen Camp mass graves 1.

Entrance to Belsen Camp.

Chapter Nineteen.

THE OFFICIAL ACCOUNT OF HANS'S ESCAPE

The Official Report of Events during and after the battle of Sidi Rezegh, 23rd November 1941

This is the personal account of Captain Hans Freund (known in the army as Harold Friend)

While stationed at Mersa Matruck with SA 5th Bde HQ, I was given 10 days' leave on 28th October 1941. I returned on 6th Nov to find that my Brigade had moved while I was away. By travelling with various supply and water convoys, I eventually managed to reach the B Schelon of the 5th Bde somewhere off the Siva Road on 11th Nov. I reported to the Brigadier, who instructed me to attach myself to the 'A' Office, in readiness for intelligence work, in particular translating, interpreting and interrogation of prisoners.

When the German Tank attack started on the B Sheldon of the 5th Bde in the afternoon of 23rd Nov, I was near my truck, which I had just moved into position on the left flank, following instructions to get the lorries into convoy formation. At about 1545 hours, I was hit by shrapnel which penetrated my left foot near the ankle. Shortly afterwards, the German tank came right among us and at approx. 1630 hours we had to surrender, together with other Bde HQ personnel. We were marched to a concentration point about a mile away from the battlefield.

On arrival, I was given a field dressing by one of our captured medical orderlies and spent the night in the open, together with the rest of the captured officers and men. There I met Maj Ollermans, Captains May and Tasker, and others of the 5th Bde HQ. When a German officer came round, asking for interpreters, I was careful not to volunteer, feeling that my knowledge of the enemy's language might prove more useful later on.

The next morning (24th Nov), Brigadier Armstrong was brought along by the Germans and allowed to address us for a few minutes. Afterwards, he came up to me and enquired after my wound. When I told him that I was only lightly wounded and hoped to get along and stay together with the other 5th Bde Officers, he advised me, rather, to try and stay behind with the wounded, advice for which I was later very grateful, because it gave me the chance to get away afterwards, whilst the others who were marched off the same morning are still in enemy hands.

In the afternoon, when only the wounded were left, the Germans took us, together with Lt-Col Melzer of the 11th 7d Ambulance, to where they thought were their Div. HQ. However, NZ troops had taken the position in the morning, and when we got there we were fired on. The German staff car that led our little convoy thereupon made off, leaving us to be rescued by the New Zealanders.

Next morning (25th Nov), we wounded were to be sent to a 7d Hospital near the frontier. Maj Walker (OC 5th Bde W/Shops) was in charge of the convoy. After we had passed 13th Corps HQ late in the afternoon, we ran in the darkness into an enemy armoured column, turned tail and hurried back. This happened several times,

Chapter Nineteen. The Official Account of Hans's Escape

until we eventually got back to the same NZ camp again on the 27th. Ambulance (Maj Melzer) was also in this camp and I attached myself to them, occasionally interpreting when German PoW casualties were being treated (e.g. on the 27th, a convoy of German ambulances drove into our camp, under a staff doctor ('Stabsarzt Neul'), gave itself up and asked for treatment, which was given).

On Friday 28th Nov, at 1700 hrs, a large German motorised column approached the camp from the south, released some 350 German PoWs, whom we had kept there, and took possession of the whole camp. We were prisoners for the second time.

After a couple of days, the Germans handed us over to the Italians and things became rather difficult. Food and water were short, and the wounded could not be treated properly owing to lack of medical supplies. Furthermore, the Italians brought their guns right up to the edge of the camp, thus affecting our own artillery fire.

Sunday the 30th, a shell from our own side burst onto the tent in which I and other wounded SA officers were lying (including Lts B. Morrison, Asher and Patterson, all of the 3TS), killing 2 NE's and one European OR. After that, we moved to open slit trenches.

By that time, I was able to walk about slowly and pick up information from German troops passing through the camp. Whenever I spoke to them, I assumed a broken accent. When asked where I had picked up my German, I used to say from a German family that lived next door to us in Pretoria. Actually, of course, I understood much more than they thought I could and passed on to our senior officers such information as I obtained, e.g. it was clear from their conversation that they evacuated their own wounded by air from Al-Adeni, until one day I heard them say that the road to Al-Adeni was no longer safe for them, which gave all those of us who toyed with the idea of escaping a useful hint in which direction to go.

As the days went on, the firing ceased, and our hopes of being relieved began to dwindle, because our own troops seemed further away now. The enemy began to round up medical personnel and walking wounded to take them away to the rear. On 1st Dec, the first batches, totalling 200 to 300, were removed in large Italian lorries.

Gradually, my foot improved, and I was fortunate in joining a group of New Zealand officers and men determined in attempting to escape. There was a lorry in the camp from which someone had removed the distributor, thereby immobilising it and rendering it useless to the enemy. We had the distributor and managed to collect a small quantity of petrol and water. I collected Sgt N. J. Lawrence of the 4th SA RMT Cg, who helped in these secret preparations. The senior officer of our party was Lt-Col (now Maj-Gen) Kippenberger, OC 20th NZ Btn and also a PoW.

It was decided to use the lorry and make a dash for it during the night of 3rd Dec. Unfortunately, however, our plans were frustrated when, late in the afternoon, an Italian armed column, including at least 50 tanks, drove up to the southern end of the camp, dispersed and stopped there. We held a meeting and decided to postpone the attempt to the following night, hoping that the Italian column would have moved by then.

Meanwhile, time was pressing, because our jailers kept rounding up our men and sending them further back behind their lines, and we never knew when our turn might come. So, when it appeared next morning (4th Dec) that the armed column had moved during the night and the way to the South was now clear as far as I could make out, half of us of the original party decided to wait no longer, but attempt to escape right now in daylight.

Between 1000 hours and 1130 hours, eighteen officers and men, one by one, climbed onto the back of the lorry, hiding under blankets.

Unfortunately, just then the Italian Camp Commandant came around, searching for any available transport. He looked at our lorry, which he assumed to be disabled, but which by that time held already 14 officers and men. I and others of us who were still outside came forward and managed to distract his attention from the lorry by telling him of some wounded Italians in a nearby tent, and taking him there. A few guards who came around were similarly dealt with and I took a number of them into the same tent to the same wounded Italians.

All was quiet now, and we decided that I should sit in front of the lorry, next to the driver, and with my knowledge of German try to bluff my way through if we should be stopped. I wore my own dilapidated greatcoat, an Italian Balaclava Helmet and had a German cap with me. (The driver of the lorry himself could not be seen so clearly, as his side was closed up by a dusty canvas-cellophane window, whilst my side was quite open to enable me to get a clear view of the terrain).

At 1115 all seemed ready. Lt-Col (Maj-Gen) Kippenberger was the last to get into the back of the truck and then I jumped on to the front seat. We started. So as not to attract any undue attention, I did not let the driver go fast, but we moved very slowly and in second gear all the time. The guards, naturally, saw us, but did not appear to find anything wrong in what they took to be one of their own lorries with their own drivers moving slowly and in broad daylight out of the camp.

It was more or less the direction which the Italian traffic usually took. But as soon as we were out of sight of the camp, I turned due south and put on speed, avoiding small groups of enemy transport all the time. Gradually, we got away from the camp and the isolated groups around it, and now raced through the desert.

All went well for approx. 10 miles, when we suddenly came across a widely dispersed formation of armoured vehicles. That was a bitter disappointment. Turning back now would have meant certain recapture; so, having taken so many chances that day, I decided to take one more, and try to get through the column, driving very slowly and hoping these tanks and armoured cars would take no notice of an isolated and unarmed lorry.

However, as soon as we got into their range they opened fire on us. Our lorry was hit twice by shell splinters, one of which struck the floor between my feet, missing them by inches. There was nothing to do but to stop, get out and once more (third time!) surrender.

When the first armoured car came up to us, I addressed the gunner in German, starting to tell him a story which we had prepared in advance (i.e. that we had left the prison camp because the Italians would not give our wounded sufficient water, and that we had come out in search of some Germans to appeal to them against the Italians' injustice).

I had hardly spoken the first few words of the touching tale when a broad Cockney voice interrupted and asked: 'Are you Jerries?' We had struck an advanced patrol of British vehicles and surrendered to our own people.

An escort took us to the OC, to whom we gave information regarding the exact position of the camp from which we had escaped. The next day, Lt-Col Kippenberger and two majors from our party interviewed Brigadier 'Jock' Campbell VC/OC. I subsequently heard that the 'cage' was recaptured by our troops a few days later and that approx. 100 of the original 1000 PoWs were rescued.

Chapter Nineteen. The Official Account of Hans's Escape

Travelling by convoy and Hospital Trains, I had by that time reached No 6 General Hospital.

The following are the names of the officers included in our escape:

Lt-Col H. K. Kippenberger	(OC 20th NZ Btn)
Capt J. A. T. Rhodes	(Adj 20th NZ Btn)
Lt C. S. Pepper	(7 Anti Tk Rgt, NZ)
2-Lt A. P. Boyle	(20th NZ Btn)
Major Wilson	(NZ Mobile Surgical Unit)
Major Lovell	(5 NZ Field Ambulance)
Capt D. Jack	(4 NZ Field Ambulance)
2-Lt B. Jackson	(18 NZ Btn) and
Sgt N. J. Lawrence	(4 South Afr RMT, att. 5th Bde)

Captain H. Freund
18th June 1944 Potchefstroom

The above is a copy made from the draft of the original report, handed to Lt-Col Malherbe? January 1942

Chapter Twenty.

OUR BABY DAVID IS BORN

Two days before the baby was due, I returned to my flat. My good friend Margaret Tasman (later married and became Margaret Rainey) came to stay with me. I don't know who recommended the specialist – I think he was Dutch and his name was De Groen. I knew very little about childbirth and no one enlightened me. There were no birth training classes in those days, but I do remember going to the Library to get a few books from the Fiction section that I foolishly thought I could read and enjoy while in labour.

This shows you how little I knew. At twelve midnight on the very day when the baby was due, my labour pains started. My friend Margaret took me into the Moedersbond Maternity Hospital by taxi. The welcome I received there was not of the happiest.

'Oh,' said the Registrar with a smile, 'a German name.' They seemed to approve of that. This confirmed my view that there were many people, particularly Afrikaners, who remembered the Boer War and were not too fond of English people. They favoured the German side in the war.

At long last I was taken to a special room, where I was suitably clad in a hospital gown and more or less left on my own for what seemed like a very long time. After many hours, when the baby was due to arrive, I was taken into the special delivery room and

Chapter Twenty. Our baby David is born

then instructed as to what to do. In the final stages of labour, I was given gas to inhale and the baby was born. I was unconscious at the end, but then I woke to find the most beautiful baby boy you can imagine – with a big head and a lot of hair.

Quite soon, Margaret Tasman appeared – she had been in the waiting room for some time. She, too, had a story to tell. She had gone to her Nursery School as usual and at about half past ten had rung up to enquire how I was faring. 'Oh,' was the reply, 'she has just had a lovely little boy.'

She left school, bought some flowers and sent two telegrams: one to my family in London and the other to Hans in Cairo to tell that we had a little boy. When she arrived at the Moedersbond Maternity Hospital, they said: 'Oh, no – she's in the final stages of labour.' How would it be if she had to send off two more telegrams – to say it is not a boy but a girl? No father could have paced the floor more anxiously than she did, but all was well in the end – because a boy had been born. I stayed in the hospital for a full two weeks. The babies were kept in a Nursery – not with their mothers – and you would hear the cries as the nurses brought them along on a trolley to be fed. After the two weeks, I hired a nurse to come and stay with me for another fortnight. I think this was a sensible move and she was a great help. After ten days, I had a phone call from Hans, who had just arrived in Durban from Cairo. He had not received the telegram and I had to tell him that I was delivered of a little baby boy. When the nurse knew that he was coming, she said that she did not want to stay because it made her too sad to think of her husband, who was still up North with the army.

When Hans was due to come back from the war, I was alone with the baby for the first time. This may account for the fact that I was too anxious to leave the baby with anyone or to take the baby with me, and I waited for Hans to arrive at the flat.

He arrived on the doorstep and my first concern was to show him the baby. I said: 'Come and see the baby. Come and see our baby.'

He said: 'First, let me see you.' And then, at last, we were united, and he looked at this little new-born baby who was lying quietly in his cot.

We move to Kimberley

After two weeks' holiday, Hans was drafted temporarily to the Army camp outside Pretoria, but he was still able to come home of an evening. Very soon, he was told that his next post would be in Kimberley at an Army camp, where RAF men were flown out from England to be trained as air pilots. Hans said he would try and find accommodation for baby David and myself as soon as possible. Not long after that, he returned to tell us he had found a place for us in Kimberley, and once again we sub-let the flat.

We slept overnight on the train and arrived in Kimberley, which is about halfway between Johannesburg and Cape Town, and it seemed rather remote.

Kimberley I found to be a very well set out town, with wide tree-lined streets and good shops. Kimberley owed its origins to the famous diamond mines.

Hans had found us accommodation with Doctor Sol Hen and his wife, who came from Manchester. They had a little baby girl, a few weeks older than David. They had given us a very large room with two beds that led to the dining room and kitchen, at the back of the house. It was a big house and they made us very welcome, but I do remember how very cold it seemed after Pretoria. Through Mrs Hen, I met members of the Kimberley Jewish community. I

Chapter Twenty. Our baby David is born

remember one very kind family invited us for the Seder. Another interesting woman, a widow, was a German refugee, and she offered us much hospitality. Hans particularly enjoyed her German, Jewish-style meals.

One recipe I learnt from her and used frequently for many years was Topside of Beef soaked in vinegar for two days and then roasted in the oven with ginger, served with a thick sauce made of ginger-nut biscuit and capers. We loved this recipe. I should not forget to tell you that there was one man from Liverpool who I remember as having a tremendously loud voice. He, too, made us more than welcome.

Then Hans found us a little house that we could rent. It was quite near to the Synagogue. The house had a small front and back garden, with an orange tree near the gate. Inside was a sitting room, one bedroom, a kitchen and a primitive type of bathroom and toilet which was at the end of the garden. One good point was that it had an enclosed stoep (veranda), where David could crawl about.

I soon met Hans's fellow officers from the Army. Most important of all, two people who became our dear friends for the rest of their lives: Abe Adelstein and his new wife Cynthia, a very beautiful young woman. Abe was a medical doctor, working in what was then called the Coloured Regiment (mixed-race men). It is important to note that the mixed-race men of this regiment were not allowed to bear arms. We saw a great deal of Abe and Cynthia and had much in common. I remember that Cynthia organised a shop where goods could be sold in aid of Russia, our new allies.

We had two interesting friends visiting us while in Kimberley. The first was Margaret Tasman and her friend Constance Stuart, an outstanding photographer, who took photographs which I still have of baby David. They had come by train for the weekend to see if I was all right. I think that it was on this occasion that Margaret told me that she had become engaged to Reg Rainey, who was then in charge of the weather forecasts, working for the Army.

The second visit was from my cousin Kenneth Stern. He and my cousin George, being both from Liverpool, were now Captains of two small naval vessels called corvettes. Kenneth had come up the coast by train to Johannesburg to meet Dr Lowenthal and then came on to stay with us in Kimberley. I believe his corvette had been sent to sink a German boat floating somewhere off Simonstown. He stayed with us for a day or two and even gave a little talk on Naval matters at Abe and Cynthia's home.

We stayed in Kimberley for at least a year until Hans was posted to a new place called Potchefstroom. Once Hans had found accommodation for us, we joined him.

Potchefstroom

When David was about two and a half years old, Hans was transferred to a large South African army camp in Potchefstroom, in the Transvaal. This was a small country town halfway between Kimberley and Johannesburg. If I remember rightly, there was only one main shopping centre. Hans rented a charming bungalow. In fact, most of the houses where we stayed both in Kimberley and in Potchefstroom had only one storey. This house was spacious and well built. It had a big lawn in front with a garden. You entered it by a large stoep (veranda), a very pleasant place to sit. I will never forget the pleasure of leaning over the side of the small wall to pick a delicious nectarine which had been warmed by the sun.

Along all the roads ran a wide gutter filled with flowing water. At a certain time, each week, we were permitted to lift the little barrier and let the water run into our own garden. When David was old

Chapter Twenty. Our baby David is born

enough, I remember he took off his shoes and let them float away in the water.

The town was surrounded by green pastures and many householders seemed to own their own cow, and you would see these cows walking back to their own homes, unaccompanied, in the evening. On one occasion a cow walked into our garden and ate all the dahlias, before I could chase her out. The house had every amenity except for the toilet, which was the usual primitive arrangement in the garden. At some stage a proper toilet was installed, which was a great improvement.

Hans worked nearby, as Information Officer at a large Army camp. He rode there by bicycle each day. Potchefstroom was so flat that bicycles were useful. For the first time I was able to satisfy an old ambition of mine, which was to own and ride a bicycle. While I learnt this skill, I remember falling off quite dramatically in front of a whole Army van of soldiers, who cheered me on, much to my embarrassment.

I did not meet many of the town folk, but made friends with the wives and officers from Hans's headquarters. Many of the wives lived alone, as their husbands were stationed away in North Africa. It's a good thing I cannot remember fully some of the goings-on whilst their husbands were away, for some of the woman had affairs with other officers. When their husbands returned from North Africa, the women all had to drop their boyfriends.

Soon after arriving in Potchefstroom, Abe and Cynthia suggested we went for the weekend, bringing little David with us, to visit Abe's mother and father. Abe's parents lived near to a town called Bethel. It was one of the most remote places I had ever visited. They had no electricity or gas. Abe had brought them a 'primus' `(a stove) as a gift. We had one that we used for frying and it could be taken anywhere. But this one, instead of providing cooking facilities, shone a bright light, which was much appreciated. I remember that night they put two upright armchairs together, where little David could sleep safely.

Abe's parents came from the Pale of Settlement in Northern Europe and, like many Jews arriving in South Africa, found they could make a good living if they settled in the more remote parts of the country. With foresight, they sent Abe to Johannesburg, so that he could study to become a doctor. After a severe illness, he eventually became a senior lecturer at Manchester University Medical School. Years later, when he was in his late fifties, he was the Under Secretary of Health at Somerset House, London, where he was in charge of Epidemiology. He invited Hans and me to visit his grand office overlooking the Thames. What an amazing achievement from such a remote home where he was a young boy living in South Africa.

To return to our time in Potchefstroom, I recall one specific occasion when visiting the Army camp. A group of entertainers was expected to come and give the soldiers a special evening of enjoyment. Many hundreds of soldiers gathered in a large tent for this performance. I sat in the front row with the officers. However, the entertainers were delayed for some reason and the soldiers then became restless.

I was surprised to see Hans walk onto the stage and without any fuss sit himself down at the piano. He accompanied himself, sang out in a strong voice and encouraged everyone to join in with the singing of some popular songs. We sang well-known South African numbers: *'Sarie Maria Daar Kom die Alibama'*, *'Oh die Kat kom veer'* and Army songs such as *'Hang out the Washing on the Siegfried Line'* and *'Lili Marlene'*. This went on for at least twenty minutes, with everyone joining in most heartily until the entertainers arrived. I was very proud of him.

Chapter Twenty. Our baby David is born

I start a new Teaching Post

Our house was quite near the railway, which ran from Cape Town to Johannesburg. If you wanted to go by train to Johannesburg, you could walk to the station, where there were two carriages, in a siding. If you went in the evening you would find bunks prepared for you to use and one could undress and go to sleep in one of these bunks until the morning. In the middle of the night, the main train coming from Cape Town would stop and attach the Potchefstroom carriages. After much shunting, one would set off for Johannesburg. Even if you awoke with all this noise, you would soon be asleep again as the train went on its way.

We travelled this way a number of times. One time, baby David and I went to Pretoria and stayed with Margaret Tasman, now Mrs Rainey. She had become much more affluent after her marriage. We had already met Reg when we lived in Pretoria. He was in charge of a research station, improving the quality of wheat. I remember one day Hans met him early in the morning. Hans had just bought two delicious cakes from a wonderful bakery called Turkstrais. They were far more tempting than anything you found in London. 'I am going to have these for my breakfast,' said Hans.

'What a splendid idea,' said Reg, and proceeded to do the same.

Reg was born in the north of England and had gone to either Oxford or Cambridge. He had done this entirely on his own merit. During the war, as I have already said, he was in charge of weather forecasts for the Army. Many years later, when he was in charge of world locust control, he became a member of the Royal Society, which is a great honour in England.

My visit to Pretoria gave me the opportunity to see my old friends the Zways, who were now living in a grander house. Margaret had introduced me to friends who were working with Reg, the Schaffers. Walter Schaffer had been a senior lecturer in Natal. I remember this meeting with Gladys and Walter. Their elder daughter Donna stood alongside her father. She was about twelve and their two younger sons, Herman and Benjamin, were there, too. We all became life-long friends.

About a year later, I was offered a post to be in charge of a little nursery school which was run by the local authorities in a park nearby. It suited me very well and the hours were from 9am to mid-day. It was only a few minutes away and I rode my bicycle, with David perched on a little seat behind me, putting his arms around my waist. No helmets in those days, of course, and I repeated all the time, 'Keep your feet out. Keep your feet out.' David must have been about two and a half years old.

At about 11am each day, my helper arrived with a pram to fetch David to take him home to have his morning sleep. This particular helper had come with me from Kimberley. Her appearance was unlike the people of 'mixed race' and she was probably descended from the Bushman people. She was very small, pale-faced, with a very large behind. She was probably in her late thirties. She was a very sensible and helpful person, but eventually returned to Kimberley. This nursery school had failed the expected standard school test, but I was soon able to make improvements.

Chapter Twenty-One.

THE WAR ENDS. OUR BABY ERICA IS BORN

The years passed and now it looked as if we were winning the war. Throughout the war, for security reasons, Hans adopted the name Harold Friend, rather than the German name of Hans Freund. After the war, we had considered changing our name from Freund to Friend and went through all the processes required, but it was refused by the South African authorities. We decided not to bother and stuck to Freund, which I do not regret. I suppose they thought the more German-sounding name of Hans Freund was preferable.

I never neglected sending letters home to the family in London. Sometimes, because of war regulations, these letters had to be short, but I kept in contact with my family nevertheless. Aunt Esther and Myer had now purchased the lower half of a house in Inverness Terrace, next door to their hotel. This was very convenient for them as the cook from the hotel was able to make their meals. They stayed in London throughout the Blitz, which must have been a great strain and worry. I remember they told me about the last of Hitler's weapons, known as the Doodlebug. These planes were launched without any personnel aboard and when the sound switched off you knew it was coming down, probably near you, which was very frightening.

Throughout the war, members of my family were involved. I've already told you that my cousin Kenneth came to see us in South Africa and that he and his brother George were captains of corvettes, which were small warships. They both took part in the famous and dangerous rescue at Dunkirk; and later George was posted to the Mediterranean to join the war effort.

My cousin Marcus was a pilot and prisoner of war during the First World War. In about 1936, the Royal Air Force encouraged former pilots to retrain. This Marcus did. As soon as war was declared, he was one of the very first to be called up. He was put in charge of a squadron. He has written details of his work. Later, he was assigned to the famous leader Field-Marshal Montgomery and was granted the status of a Wing Commander. The Royal Air Force Museum in Hendon has a detailed account of his war experiences. He was rescued from Dunkirk with Montgomery. He was involved in the Dieppe raid and he was in France on the first day of the invasion. Eventually, he received the OBE from the Queen.

Our move to Cape Town. Working in the Jewish Orphanage

As the war drew successfully to a close, many of the South African personnel began to look for work as civilians. One day, on reading the Jewish newspaper, I noticed an advertisement. This was from the Jewish Orphanage in Cape Town, and they required a principal and matron. I thought this would suit us very well and we sent in our application. Mr Klute, the secretary, travelled to Potchefstroom to interview us. Following this, we were offered the posts. Hans then applied to leave the Army and we made our way down to the Cape. This position appealed to us because we liked Cape Town, with its attractive mountainous countryside and the sea.

Chapter Twenty-One. The War ends. Our baby Erica is born

When we arrived at Cape Town railway station, we were met by members of the Orphanage Committee and I was given a beautiful bouquet of flowers. We were driven to Oranjezicht, situated on the lower slopes of Table Mountain. The orphanage was of a fair size and the building in Montrose Avenue seemed attractive. It was situated on the highest point of the city, with the slopes of the mountain behind. We were introduced to the children, who numbered about one hundred. They were from five years of age up to sixteen or seventeen, both boys and girls. David was by now three and a half years old.

The past principal and matron had retired after working in the institution for years. Our coming was a major event. Hans at that time was known as Captain Freund, and was still in uniform. I recall there was a big hall where the children could read and play. Behind the large dining room was the kitchen, and the children's bedrooms were upstairs. We ourselves had a little flat, consisting of a bedroom, a sitting room, toilet and a very pleasant veranda.

It had a wonderful view over Table Bay. To the right was Devil's Peak, to the left Lion's Head and Signal Hill, with what we called the Squirrel Park lower down, leading to the ancient and famous Company's Garden. The main road, called De Waal Drive, followed a route along the mountain-side and beyond. One could look down on the important port, where the Union Castle liners docked. It was a breathtaking and unforgettable view. I think on the second night, after we had arrived, a great storm arose, the like of which I had never before experienced. No wonder Cape Town was known as 'The Cape of Storms'.

During this frightening tempest, you could hear the Green Point Foghorn, with its deep tones. I found the sounds comforting and reassuring. The next day the trees appeared blown about and battered, but the air was fresh and delightful.

Our life in the orphanage began, and there was plenty to keep us occupied. Fortunately, we had the services of an excellent cook and I had no worries on that score. The older children attended various schools in the neighbourhood and took a packed lunch of sandwiches and fruit with them each day.

The younger children, who remained in the home, appeared wild and unruly. The woman in charge had no training for the job and appeared to have little understanding as to how to provide for the needs of young children. I was shocked to find that they had no toys. I gave then many of my son David's toys and I saw very soon how these children destroyed them.

The orphanage had an interesting history. In former times, Mr Ochberg had gone to Poland and gathered together two hundred Jewish children who were orphans, as a result of the pogroms and the war. He was permitted to take them out of the country. First, they stayed in England, which aroused considerable interest, and the King and Queen visited them before they left for South Africa. The children were disappointed when they were not wearing crowns.

They travelled on a Union Castle liner to Cape Town. Half of these children went to the orphanage in Johannesburg, and the rest were cared for in the Cape Town Jewish Orphanage. But this was in the past, and those children had long since grown up and left. At this time, there was less of a demand for places and most of the children were from local Jewish families.

In the meantime, I received a letter from my family in London, in which Daddy Myer and Auntie Esther warned me against accepting the post in Cape Town. From their experience, they thought we would find the work difficult. I was in my first month of pregnancy, but had not told the Orphanage Committee. Fortunately, I felt better than in the previous pregnancy.

Chapter Twenty-One. The War ends. Our baby Erica is born

We enjoyed a good relationship with the children and it was clear that Hans was especially popular. Our relationship with the Managing Committee was not so easy, and, on reflection, was not entirely their fault. Certain members of the committee frequently visited to give us advice. Somebody told me that I was very young to have this post, which was, of course, not true. I was thirty-two and a qualified teacher with great personal experience of an orphanage.

Probably they were anxious about the change after having had the security of the same principal and matron for so many years. It had never occurred to me to consult Mr Klute, the secretary, when I introduced certain changes. For example, I thought that the children were not given sufficient milk to drink and made changes to the menu.

Then a bug that I had never come across before was found in one of the girl's beds in the dormitory. I did not realise that such insects were quite unusual in the Cape climate, but it horrified me, coming from England. I immediately ordered all the beds in the entire dormitory to be fumigated.

Mr Klute said, much to my surprise, that I should have simply used a spray. During the following months, I met the members of the committee, who involved themselves in the running of the orphanage. For example, there was an intelligent woman who devoted much of her time to managing the children's library. The local Jewish doctor was most supportive, as well as caring. Dr Louis Mirvish, a child specialist, visited frequently and was most helpful. A blind man, well known in the community, joined us for dinner on a Friday evening and afterwards encouraged the children to sing many modern Hebrew songs.

I met some of the neighbours, including a Mrs Landsberg, who was a refugee from Germany, and made some new friends.

I remember when David, nearly three years old, had his hair cut for the first time by the barber at the orphanage. Some of the children gathered round to watch, the girls exclaiming, 'What a shame!' as his red-haired locks were cut away.

At the weekend, most of the children were taken out by their relations for the afternoon. This meant we were free and could go for a walk to De Waal Park, which was lower down the slopes of Table Mountains. The hills were very steep and as you descended I remember little David turning around, looking over his shoulder and asking, 'Who's pushing me?'

Another beautiful walk was going through the gap in the mountain known as Kloof Nek, which led down to the sea at Camps Bay, on the Atlantic Ocean side.

The birth of our Baby Girl

The months passed. Shortly before my baby was due, we heard the news that Japan had capitulated to the Allies. Hans and I were with Hans's friend Arthur Greitzer, sitting outside on the veranda, celebrating this event with a glass of wine. I remember thinking: My baby will be born now into a peaceful world.

In January 1945, just before I was due to have my second baby, David became ill with a viral infection. He developed a very sore throat and high temperature. One of the doctors thought he had an infectious illness and, chiefly because of its possible danger to the other children, he was sent to the fever hospital in Mouille Point on the foreshore.

I said to David, 'I'm going into hospital soon to have a little baby. Would you like to go into hospital?' And he agreed, on condition

Chapter Twenty-One. The War ends. Our baby Erica is born

that he could take one of his special toys with him that had been sent from Israel by my cousin Harold. He was not allowed to bring it out again, much to his regret.

Perhaps two days later, my labour started, and Hans took me with my packed bag to a nursing home in Tamberskloof, not too far away. I had already booked a place there. I remember Hans running along with the suitcase, while I walked slowly behind him. This was a new experience for him, as he had been up north when David had been born. I was received with kindness, and this was quite different to my experience before when giving birth in Pretoria at The Moedersbond.

I was examined carefully, and the doctor announced that there was plenty of time and that he could go home and would advise the father to do likewise. In those days, fathers were not allowed into the labour ward. However, as soon as the doctor arrived home, he was asked to come back immediately as my labour had progressed quickly. The doctor and the nurse assisted in the delivery of my new baby: a girl with pretty red hair.

Thinking that Hans had gone home, the doctor said; 'You had better ring the father.'

'He is still in the waiting room,' they replied. 'He did not go home.'

'Of course not,' I said with pride, and all I remember was that I felt very tired and Hans was worried that we needed to be on time to put the notice of the birth in the local *Jewish Chronicle*. It was a busy time for Hans because David was due to leave the fever hospital, but the good news was that David did not have a contagious illness. Nevertheless, because of the risk of infection, Hans did not bring him to see me at the nursing home, where I was staying.

So, life continued at the orphanage, but I felt unhappy with what I thought was the amount of interference by members of the committee. I remember one evening somebody rang us up very late, whilst we were going to bed, to enquire how much we were paying for apples. Somehow that finished me off and I suggested to Hans that we should give up this position. I think we had been in the job for about a year. We gave a month's notice, despite at the time having nowhere to go.

Our move to Strand

Hans managed to find a cottage in Strand, a beautiful seaside resort not far from Cape Town. When we left the orphanage, Hans was still under the protection of the forces, because it was only a year after he was demobbed. This meant that his Army wages were reinstated, and that was a great help.

The cottage was in an attractive position, almost facing the sea. Opposite, were delightful little rock pools, which David delighted in exploring. The cottage had a bedroom, a sitting room and a kitchen and some sort of a bathroom. The toilet was a primitive bucket system and was most unpleasant. I remember going to the cinema, which was close by, rather than use our own toilet. Once we had settled in, Hans made a trip to Johannesburg, hoping to find work.

The Jewish Board of Deputies in Johannesburg gave him some temporary employment. I found a pleasant young girl to help me, and while I was busy in the mornings with baby Erica, she would take David to play in the rock-pools by the sea. I think David's health improved and he looked much stronger. I remember Mrs Landsberg came to visit me to see how I was managing. When Hans returned, he had found work outside Cape Town in a place called Tokai. This was a large forest on the slopes of Constantia Mountain, in which two

Chapter Twenty-One. The War ends. Our baby Erica is born

reformatory schools were situated. The institutions were segregated – one for the white boys and another for the coloured (mixed-race) male pupils. Hans taught at the mixed-race reformatory.

We were offered a cottage, part of a row provided for the teachers. We were given this for only six months, as the original occupant and his family were on leave in Holland. The situation was unusual for me. It was very remote, although a public bus did pass the door now and again. Most of the teachers were Afrikaans-speaking. But the government had asked public servants to take in Army personnel and so help them return to civilian life.

I remember the Afrikaans woman next door being amazed when I told her that I wasn't that interested in cooking. She, of course, was an expert; and, like many Afrikaans wives, had rows and rows of bottled fruit that she had prepared herself.

Soon after this, my mother in London wrote that she was coming out to see me. On reflection, this was a brave action, as the Union Castle ships had not been re-converted back from being troop ships used in the war, and people had to sleep in hammocks.

We went to meet her in the harbour when she arrived and took her back with us to stay in our home in Tokai. She was shocked to see how I was living and although it was very beautiful, she was used to living in a city. I remember she said she would like to wheel Erica in her pram around the block and I said there was no such thing as a block. She had brought beautiful clothes with her for herself, and I remember a particular hat which was festooned with flowers and cherries. Little Erica, although she was only three, was greatly taken with this special hat. She said she wanted to wear it, and when we suggested a less expensive, simpler hat, she threw the hat we offered her onto the ground, demanding the more elaborate, ornate one. I have a picture of Erica walking ahead, wearing her grandmother's hat.

My mother, enterprising as ever, soon got in touch with people she knew, like Mrs Goodman and one or two other friends she knew from Liverpool. I had not seen my mother since I had left England in 1938. Eight years had passed since we had been together. She enjoyed taking David regularly to the Rondebosch Arts Centre in the suburb of Cape Town, and that was a splendid experience for him.

I remember on one occasion there had been a shipwreck on the rocks quite near Cape Town and we drove out to see it. It was quite a sight to see this broken boat, with cargo floating around in the water. Before my mother returned to London, she wished to give us some bedroom furniture, and we bought a beautiful bed, a chest of drawers and a cupboard made from the wood Emboya, a South African hard wood. Before my mother returned to England, I promised her that I would soon bring the children to London on a visit.

Our move to Pollsmoor Village

After six months, we had to leave the Tokai cottage and were rehoused in Pollsmoor village, which was nearby. It had been an army camp, but was converted into bungalows for the ex-Army personnel. These single-storey bungalows were mostly made of corrugated iron sheeting. Inside, they were well fitted out with wooden floors. We had a lounge, a kitchen, a modern bathroom and two bedrooms. It was a large village. We were all ex-servicemen with their families. The bungalows were not particularly well ventilated, being either too hot or too cold. It was very safe and we all felt quite comfortable with each other.

Later, these corrugated iron bungalows that had been a village for ex-servicemen was closed, and after many years it became the prison where Nelson Mandela was held during the final stages of his imprisonment.

Chapter Twenty-One. The War ends. Our baby Erica is born

In Pollsmoor village we met again Dr and Mrs Schaffer and their three children Dona, Herman and Benjamin, whom we had met in Pretoria, as well as Ludwig Freed, who had been in the South African Army. His mother had come from Israel to live with him. We made many good friends when we lived in the village.

Pollsmoor village is on the outskirts of Cape Town. It is some distance from the railway and the nearest station was called Retreat. It was not far from Muizenberg beach and surrounded by the beautiful Cape Town mountains. There were not many cars and therefore it was a safe environment where the children could play. Everyone had something in common: they had all experienced being in the war. There were no shops in Pollsmoor and you had to go into Retreat to buy whatever you needed or to a very good grocer shop on the Ladies Mile road nearby.

Later, when Hans and I were both earning, we could afford to buy a washing machine with a mangle, as well as a splendid refrigerator. Both of these domestic appliances were extremely useful and fairly new to South Africa.

Now I was ready to keep my promise to my mother to visit London to see the family. Hans took me, the children and at least thirteen cases, including a doll's pram, a tricycle and many other items, and we boarded a Union Castle ship set for England. We had arranged to have a cabin to ourselves for the journey.

As soon as we left Cape Town, I was very seasick and left the children on deck, but another kind passenger brought them down to me. During the voyage the children were not allowed to eat with the adults. I had to eat in the adult dining room and I sat with a very disagreeable couple at a round table, with no one else to talk to. I had to leave the children either in the noisy nursery or playing quite safely in our cabin by themselves. One day, they managed to throw all their little tyres from the Dinky toys out of the porthole. After I'd eaten, I then had to take David and Erica for their meal. All this seemed to occupy a great deal of the time.

When we reached Madeira, we were not allowed to disembark, but many traders came on board and I bought quite a few nice presents, including a large bunch of bananas and orchids. A few days later, we arrived in Southampton. We stood looking over at the quayside and, at first, I could not see my Aunt Annie. Eventually, I lifted Erica up so that she could look out and as soon as Aunt Annie saw her copper hair, she shouted a welcome to us.

In no time we had left the boat and found seats on the train, which was nearby, and which would take us to London. Auntie Annie suggested that we go and have a cup of tea in the train's dining carriage. This was a very grand tea, including sandwiches and cakes. By the time it was finished, the train arrived in Euston Station, London. At this time, Erica was about two and a half and David five years old. The journey from Cape Town to Southampton had taken fourteen days.

My cousin Marcus was waiting on the platform. It took some time to get all our various cases together and Auntie Annie and I and the two children left Marcus to cope with the luggage whilst we went off in a taxi to Inverness Terrace. You can imagine the excitement. My aunt and uncle were living next door and occupied the lower half of one of the three houses that formed the hotel. My mother had hired a nurse and a rather large perambulator.

I remember seeing Marcus the next morning pushing Erica in the pram in Kensington Gardens, with the nurse by his side. Marcus was so excited. During the whole of our stay it was wonderful to be so near these beautiful gardens, which were across the road from the hotel. David would ride helter-skelter on his tricycle, unlike other children, who would ride sedately with their nurses or parents. He also frequently climbed the trees, as he was used to doing this in Tokai forest. He did this much to Marcus's admiration.

On the second day, Daddy Myer, a retired headmaster, felt that it was important for David to go to school. Daddy Myer was a governor at the Bayswater Jewish School near to the Portobello Market. He took David on the bus and he was put into a class suitable for his age. In the afternoon, the headmaster brought him back to us. David was very happy indeed at this school and always thought of it fondly. I think he felt very much at home in a Jewish school and with a very understanding teacher in charge.

Chapter Twenty-Two.

A VISIT TO THE FAMILY IN LONDON

When I look back on these months that we spent in London, the most enduring memory I have is the pleasure that the whole family felt when we were all together. Everybody loved having David and Erica, and it was obvious the children gave them much joy. It was good for the children to have this relationship with their aunts, uncles and grandmother. My cousins Harold and George were living on the opposite side of the road in a mews and also came to visit.

The year before, I had suffered from a very painful backache. It started when I decided to send my family a present of a very large cake. My backache started after I carried the cake to the post office.

I attended the Groote Schuur Hospital in Cape Town, but they did not help me. Dr Halford, the son of Mrs Halford from Liverpool, who I had already met, was a great support. He was a specialist and put me into a plastic corset that I couldn't take off for two months and then, for another few weeks, into one that could be done up and undone. By the time I reached England, my back was very much better, but I had to be careful. My mother took me to a specialist, who suggested that I have a back operation. My mother was absolutely against this and took me instead to a Red Cross clinic. This clinic

Chapter Twenty-Two. A visit to the Family in London

gave me long sessions of radiotherapy and the backache finally went. Now and then, in times of stress, this backache returned.

The second event I recall entailed a visit to Liverpool and Ireland. I left Erica quite happily with my mother and aunt, much to their joy. Auntie Annie, David and myself took the train to Liverpool and over the Mersey to West Kirby, where my Aunt Clara was now living by the sea. David enjoyed playing nearby, where there was a series of small boats. After this, we went to Belfast, Ireland, by boat, and for once I wasn't seasick, and we slept overnight in two private cabins. Uncle Louis met us at the docks and we went to stay with him and his wife Annie in a rather large, attractive house. Uncle Louis had left Leeds and was now working in Belfast.

Annie was unfortunately crippled with severe arthritis. Ruth, their daughter, was now grown-up, working as an architect for Belfast municipality. She was well dressed and attractive. After returning to London, I received a letter from Hans containing a piece from a local Cape Town paper advertising a nursery school post for someone to be in charge of the school under the auspices of the Buxton Training College (later called Berkeley House). This nursery school was in Pollsmoor and only twenty yards from our home. I applied from the UK and before leaving London I heard that I had been given the job.

A family photograph was taken by one of the hotel residents in Inverness Terrace, Bayswater. The photograph showed Marcus, myself, Auntie Annie, Auntie Esther, Uncle Myer, my mother, with David and Erica sitting on the floor in front. Erica, who was then three years old, announced to us all, 'Isn't it lucky we've got Mr Danziger?' For it was Mr Danziger who was taking the photograph.

Although I was glad to be going back to South Africa, I was sad to leave the family behind. The soft muted colours of London, the gentle climate, would be very different from colourful Cape Town.

The journey home on the Union Castle line seemed much easier than the outward journey. My mother had ordered two fancy-dress outfits to be made for David and Erica. I knew the children would be able to wear them at a special occasion during the journey. They were made of crepe paper. Erica was to be dressed as a fairy and David as Dick Whittington.

'I don't want to be a fairy,' said Erica. 'I don't want to fly away.' I explained that it was only make-believe. David got a prize as Dick Whittington. I had bought a toy tortoise that you could move by pressing a rubber bulb. I stuck one of the children's toy cats on top of the tortoise, and so Dick Whittington appeared with his moving cat and won a prize.

*Our honeymoon at the seaside.
South Africa*

*Hans and I on holiday in the Game Reserve.
South Africa*

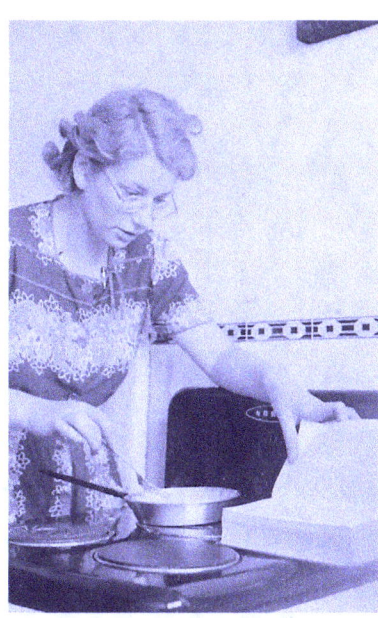

*My first attempts at cooking, using Mrs
Beaton's Cookery Book.*

1946 Cape Town. Our Family, my mother Flora, son David, daughter Erica, myself and Hans.

Baby David with his father.

Little daughter Erica on the gate of our home in Pollsmoor village.

1948 David, Erica, Aunt Esther, Daddy Myer, my mother Flora, myself, cousin Marcus and Aunt Annie.

1959 Picnic at Jonker's Hoek with my mother Flora, me, Erica, my Aunt Annie and David.

Myself, David and Erica outside our house in Eksteen Avenue, Bergvliet.

Our house in Dulton, Highstead Road Rondebosch. Erica and Hans.

Chapter Twenty-Three.

RETURN TO SOUTH AFRICA. POLLSMOOR

The Pollsmoor Nursery School

Finally, we arrived in Cape Town and there was Hans standing on the docks to meet us. He had come with a car and we returned to our bungalow in Pollsmoor village. It was a different world to the London that I had left behind.

When the schools started after the holidays, Hans rode on his bicycle up to the school in Tokai. It was safe for David to walk by himself across to the other side of the village to a rather informal primary school that had been set up for the children of Pollsmoor. When I went to the nursery school, Erica came with me. When Pollsmoor was an Army camp, this school had been the hospital. It consisted of four large bungalows arranged in a square, with a garden in the centre. The buildings had been converted to make a school. Two of the bungalows were adapted so as to provide for the children. Each bungalow consisted of a large playroom as well as a cloakroom and toilet facilities built to suit the size of small children.

In the playroom there were small tables and chairs, as well as toys such as puzzles, beads and other sensory training toys. There was also a large collection of wooden blocks. These blocks were extremely well made and even for those days quite expensive. The two remaining bungalows were fitted out as a kitchen. There was a storage room to keep the outdoor toys. Fred, the resident caretaker, had his own accommodation. The final bungalow had a small medical room, where children could be weighed, measured and given medical or nursing care. Then there was my office and more storing facilities.

In the centre was a partly grass and partly paved area with a very large sandpit, which could be covered when not in use, and a splendid climbing frame which we called a 'Jungle Gym'. This was a special demonstration nursery school for the training college. Four out of the five days, six final-year students came to work and conduct child observations.

At first, there was only one other member of staff apart from myself, but later a second teacher came to take the older children and leave me free to oversee the daily running of the school.

Each day, when the children arrived with a parent, they would be examined in the medical room to see that they were well. No child would be allowed to come into the school with a cold. The students had to learn how to care for children physically as well as in all other respects. They also learnt how to cook suitable food for children of this age. The children who attended the school were between three and six years of age. All of them came from the village and were white. The caretaker was a small, intelligent and energetic man of mixed race. I think it was his enterprise that brought into the school a bantam cock and hens and two ducks. Someone brought us a rather old donkey and I still have a photograph of Erica riding him, with Fred leading the way.

The children played every morning both inside and outside, and they listened to stories. They had their lunch at school and rested for a little time on their own canvas camp beds. Many of them slept, but were often woken by the crowing of the bantam cock, who strutted around everywhere. At 3.30pm, the children were collected, and it was time to go home.

I arranged meetings at the nursery school for the children's parents.

Holiday Time

I remember we went on an unusual holiday to the Hogs Back, far away in the Eastern Cape.

We drove along what is now called the Garden Route and stopped at the Albertinia Hotel to enjoy one of their delicious breakfasts. We stayed the night in a hotel in Port Elizabeth, before we turned inland, driving through the rolling hills of the Transkei. This was a most interesting experience. The countryside was unspoilt. We encountered the Xhosa people, living as they must have done for many generations. I remember seeing a woman carrying a heavy receptacle of water, balancing it on her head as she walked along.

We drove up country through the lovely Amatola Mountains, surrounded by lush, indigenous forest. Here was the Great Fish River, the scene of many historical frontier wars. We then continued to the Hogs Back Hotel, a comfortable, not large and simple hotel. The village of Hogs Back is at the summit of the mountain, with panoramic views. We enjoyed walking in this beautiful district.

The food was most appetising, and I remember David ate too many strawberries and came out in a rash and we had to drive him all the way to Umtata to see a doctor, who prescribed medicine for this allergy.

At night, when the children were asleep, all the adult guests played a wonderful game called *'Murder'*. It was a complicated game in which people had to discover the culprit.

After two weeks, we returned home via Grahamstown, where our friends the Schaffers had lived. We visited the town of Alice in the Transkei and the famous Fort Hare University. This was the only college where Africans could study. Many of the well-known African leaders, including Nelson Mandela, had obtained their degrees there.

Our move to Bergvliet

Hans took up a new appointment at the well-known school called The South African College School (SACS), which was situated, at that time, in the centre of Cape Town. We were able to afford a secondhand motor-car. This enabled Hans to take the long way via De Waal Drive into Cape Town. He had also taken on evening work teaching English to foreign students. He seemed to be very busy from morning to night.

The children's health had deteriorated when we lived in Pollsmoor. Our bungalow was not ventilated against extreme temperatures. It would either get very hot or very cold. I attribute this to the reason why both David and Erica were subject to colds and chest complaints. It was difficult, as I had no family to support me when the children were unwell.

It was decided that David should have his tonsils and adenoids removed at the Groote Schuur Hospital. When I went to visit him immediately after the operation, I met a young doctor on the stairs who said to me that he had to give David a blood transfusion after the operation. This was a worrying time. The children's health did not improve until we left Pollsmoor village and lived in a brick

Chapter Twenty-Three. Return to South Africa. Pollsmoor

house in Bergvliet, as opposed to a Nissan hut built of corrugated iron sheeting.

Hans joined the Jewish Ex-Service League and after that a member, Bernard Hertzberg, visited us and told us that there was a house for sale in the newly built village of Bergvliet. It was chiefly for ex-servicemen. We went to visit this house – 49 Eksteen Avenue – and we liked it very much.

The house was a detached, double-storey house, with a large garden at the front and at the back. In general, houses were single-storey. The house appealed to us and we decided to make an offer on it. I know the deposit was two hundred pounds, but we only possessed a half of this. Some good friends, Julian and Sonia Rollnick, guaranteed the outstanding amount. Even for those days, the price was very reasonable. This was the first time we lived in our own home and one that was not rented. The previous owner, who could only have been there for about eighteen months or two years, had made a large rockery garden with flowering pin-cushions and had planted wonderful proteas from seeds that he had bought from Kirstenbosch Gardens.

There was a lawn on one side and a fair amount of distance between the neighbouring houses. The back garden was adjacent to the Hertzbergs's home and we soon made a hole in the hedge so that we could climb over a sty and take the short cut to see each other. The house itself was soundly built, and if you were downstairs, you could not hear the people moving around above you. There was a lounge, dining room, three bedrooms and an upstairs bathroom, with the kitchen and servants' quarters on the ground floor. Two of the bedrooms had built-in cupboards. Through the windows of the two front bedrooms you looked out at the great Table Mountain, and from the back bedroom window, where Erica slept, there was a view of the distant mountains. A fine panorama all round.

It was a wonderful feeling to move into our own home. I cannot tell you how happy I felt when we opened the door for the very first time. This was in 1950, and Erica was five and a half years old. David was a little over eight years old.

As soon as the school term started, I made arrangements for Erica to start school. She was able to walk there quite safely on her own, together with Jeanie and Daphne Miller, who were our neighbours' children. I took the local bus to my work in Pollsmoor Nursery School. We thought that it would be good for David to go to Wynberg Boys' High School, and for the first week Herman Schaffer, the oldest of the Schaffer boys, took him there and showed him how to take the bus.

We moved all our belongings from Pollsmoor to Bergvliet and we managed to buy a dining room table and chairs which were made of 'Imboya' wood, which is a light mahogany. At first, we did not make any alterations to the house, apart from removing the unpleasant fluorescent lights.

My Mother and Aunt settle in Cape Town

Soon after we had moved, my mother and Aunt Annie came out to live in Cape Town. Daddy Myer had sold the hotel, with its remaining lease in Inverness Terrace, to a Methodist community for what we thought was a tremendous amount of money: £10,000. Some of this money went to my mother and Aunt Annie, and they decided to join us in Cape Town. We arranged that they stayed in a really attractive traditional boarding house called *India House* in Kenilworth. I remember we had Christmas dinner that year in the rather grand dining room.

My mother, however, was keen to make a home of her own. At first, they rented a furnished flat for six months, nearby. One day, while we were sitting in this new flat, my mother arrived to say that she had found a more permanent apartment in Kenwyn Mansions, on the corner of Aliwal and Kenilworth Road and the Main Road that ran between Kenilworth and Wynberg.

'Guess who lives there?' she said to David. 'Your headmaster, Mr Lorie.' David looked slightly aghast. We had sent David to Wynberg Boys' School partly because Mr Lorie, who we knew was a Jewish headmaster and a very musical man, had established an orchestra for the boys at the school. We thought this was a wonderful opportunity for David to take part in the orchestra. He was still very young, in what was called Standard Two, the second youngest class.

Kenwyn Mansions was elegant and built in the art deco style, having a magnificent garden with tall trees. Their flat was well furnished and very attractive. It made a great difference to our family to have my mother and aunt with us in Cape Town. It meant a happy situation for us all. As their flat was so near the school, David was able to go to them for lunch every day instead of taking sandwiches. My mother gave him a hot meal, ending up with two sweets, before he returned for the afternoon school session.

Very soon after Erica began as a pupil at Bergvliet Primary Junior School, she contracted mumps, and then a few days later the very serious complication of encephalitis set in. This viral infection affects the tissues surrounding the brain. We were required to admit her to the fever hospital near Cape Town.

At first, there was a nice woman in the same room with her, but later she was left there quite alone. For many years, Erica had unhappy memories about being suddenly separated from family and treated in a rigid way in the fever hospital. We all took it in turns to visit her, but were not allowed to go near her, and we could only see her through the window. Our dear Dr Louis Mirvich visited her, and Erica was comforted by his kind manner. Erica told us that he gave her tuppence and a tin of Coca Cola. When she finally returned home, she was in a highly anxious state, having been in this hospital for between two and three weeks and being kept in a situation of isolation. Erica found it traumatic to be left alone and be so ill. It took her a long time to recover from this event, and I do not think that the school and the headmaster in particular realised how this experience affected her. She took time to recover from being separated from her family and feeling ill and enduring the severity of this illness. She was only five and a half years old. The year was 1951.

I went to see the headmaster at her school, Mr Breetzke, to tell him why Erica was very anxious about being in school. Children were punished for being late, and she always ended her prayers by saying, 'Please, God, don't make me late for school'. A year later, she had her appendix out in the Catholic hospital, where the nuns were extremely kind and thoughtful.

When Hans's school moved to a new building in Newlands, he took the car and was able to drop David at his school on his way.

Our lives in Eksteen Avenue, Bergvliet

We lived in our home in Eksteen Avenue for at least six years. This was a settled time, with the children growing up, and we enjoyed the company of our increasing circle of friends. We had a dog, a cat, a rabbit and guinea-pigs that we kept in a hutch at the back of the house. We built a barbecue in the garden, behind the house.

At some stage, we bought a huge wooden crate, which we turned into a large Wendy house (nowadays called a play-house) for Erica. It had a roof, chimney, front door and window, and much play went on inside. There was a playing field nearby which gave David the opportunity to join in with games of cricket with friends.

It was quite easy to add a small room to the dining room, and this became a study for Hans.

Soon, the Nursery School authorities stopped using Pollsmoor as their demonstration Nursery School and acquired an attractive building in Newlands, where students could study and where two more demonstration schools were established. The college was now called Berkeley House, instead of the Buxton Home, although we still maintained the demonstration school at the Buxton Home. I was transferred to the nursery school within the grounds of the Buxton Home. I was in charge, together with my two assistants, Philippa Geoffrey and Helen Bourne. We three were fond of each other and worked well together.

The Nursery School was in the grounds of the Buxton Home, which was an establishment that looked after sick children. They did not take kindly to us, and so we kept our distance from them. The nursery school was purpose-built in large grounds. The children mostly came from professional families. They were brought either by their mother or father or sometimes by a nanny. A number of Jewish children attended the nursery school. As in Pollsmoor, we had students who came to observe and who gained work experience. As we were closer to the college itself, we felt more a part of the whole enterprise. These were nearly always mixed-race women. Only white children were admitted – that was in compliance with the segregation laws of the country.

The South African College School (SACS), a high school for boys, where Hans taught, had moved, and was conveniently situated near the University of Cape Town. As well as teaching German at SACS, Hans then started to lecture at Cape Town University, where he introduced a new course called Science German, which he devised to help science students.

At the SACS he introduced a Friday morning musical session for the whole school, which was quite a new feature in the curriculum. He had started this innovation before the school moved to the new site.

Every Friday morning, Hans led the entire school in communal singing. He compiled a book of verses of suitable songs that the boys could enjoy, and I have some of these books to this day. The repertoire of songs he taught were classical, folk songs in English, Afrikaans, French, German, Xhosa and Zulu. One of the African songs he taught was '*Nkosi Sikeleli Afrika*', which is today the national anthem of South Africa. When the headmaster asked what it was, Hans replied that it was an African folksong.

The headmaster objected to one of the songs, '*Drink to me only with thine eyes*', as it might encourage drinking amongst the boys.

One of the pupils, a gifted pianist, Reuben Berril, accompanied the singing on the piano. Reuben has remained a close family friend ever since and although he lives on the far side of London, he regularly came to our home to accompany Hans on the piano and Hans enjoyed so much singing the songs he loved.

At SACS, Hans was in charge of a large group of the Jewish boys whenever, in the mornings, there were religious assemblies. Later, some of these boys became well-known fighting for freedom from apartheid for the Africans in South Africa. Most notable was Albie Sachs, who eventually, as a lawyer, framed the Legal Constitution when the new South African Government came into power under President Nelson Mandela.

Chapter Twenty-Three. Return to South Africa. Pollsmoor

Hans continued to teach Science German at the university. He was elected to the Jewish Board of Deputies as a Member of the Board. When they met on a Friday, he was usually able to leave the school and attend meetings. The committee at this stage was more concerned with the plight of Israel than the Apartheid system in South Africa. Hans, as usual, was always outspoken and quite fearless in this regard, trying to get the committee to speak out against the apartheid regime. The situation in Israel was critical at this time, and so were the times in South Africa.

Friday nights and Hebrew School

Our family usually went to my mother and aunt on Friday night. We enjoyed lighting the candles, saying the blessings and having a delicious meal together. Hans sang the grace in his pleasing bass voice. After this, Hans would take David to the school nearby for orchestra practice. We had bought a cello for him on the advice of his teacher, a Mrs Hutcheson, who lived out at Simonstown, a historic naval base. This evening gave me a chance to talk to my mother and aunt.

Erica usually spent the time dressing up in all sorts of interesting items of clothing she found in my mother's wardrobe and would entertain us with poetry and songs. On the way home, we stopped in Wynberg at a fruit shop run by Asians, the Patels, and bought all our fruit and vegetables for the week. I remember they told Hans how they were being harassed by the new nationalist government. Hans encouraged them to write it all down. 'One day,' he said, 'you will get redress.'

On one occasion on the way home, there was a fair where there was a large ferris wheel. This was not something that appealed to me, but Hans went with David and Erica and sat on one of the seats.

When the seat reached the highest spot, something went wrong and there they were, stranded! A bit nerve-wracking! Hans had his arms tightly around the children, but he kept them calm and eventually they all returned safely to ground level.

In Bergvliet, where did we buy our food? There were four shops in one unit itself and we supported two. The first was a very good chemist and the second was run by a Jewish ex-serviceman. His wife was a hairdresser and her salon occupied the first floor. He kept the ground floor for stationery, books and newspapers. They called their shop 'Pages and Perms', and when you rang them on the phone they would answer, 'Pages and Perms, good afternoon.'

Most of the meat that we bought was sent directly from the heart of the Karoo, from a Mr Jackson of Beaufort West. It came by train in a hessian bag and was thrown onto the platform as the train raced by without stopping. We would drive to Heathfield station to pick it up off the platform in the evening. One week we had leg of lamb, the other week the shoulder. The hessian canvas bag was then thrown away. Today, people would be shocked by the casual way that it was delivered, but nothing untoward ever happened to us. Our groceries still came from the same grocer, Mr Eckowitz, who we used when we lived in Pollsmoor Village. The shop was in an isolated spot and was quite different to the self-service shops you have nowadays.

Our home help, called Frances, was an excellent cook. Her little daughter had the same name of Frances and lived with her, in our house, which was against the apartheid laws. Erica would play with little Frances. This little girl was not allowed to go to school with Erica, but stayed at home with her mother. Again, this was because of the apartheid laws.

Every Saturday morning, Hans took David and Erica to the Temple Israel Reform Synagogue in Greenpoint. Rabbi Sherman was from Cincinnati, in the United States.

On Saturday mornings, Auntie Annie would wait at the corner, ready for Hans to stop the car and take her with David and Erica to the Hebrew School. Auntie Annie taught the younger children. There were a great number of children attending the Saturday morning class before the shul service. The Hebrew School began with an assembly taken by Hans, and all the children sang Hebrew songs, with Auntie Annie accompanying on the piano.

Some songs were traditional, some were put to new words, and one was a new school song composed by Hans and myself:

'Haifa, Tel Aviv, Jerusalem are the houses of our school ... hardly ever are we late, we're learning ... etc.'

This was followed by two religious classes.

Family Days Out

Every Sunday, my mother and aunt came to us for the day, and when the weather was fine, we went out to some of the beautiful places around Cape Town. We both worked quite hard in those days and Hans in particular. He taught English to foreigners at the Technical College on Monday and Wednesday evenings. He also did quite a lot of private teaching. Quite a few Barmitzvah boys learned their portion from Hans, and he taught a number of adults English and pupils German for Matriculation. Of these I shall just mention two. One was Mr Chaub of Rex Trueform, which was a large firm that manufactured men's clothes. From then on, Hans always bought his clothes and David's from this wholesale source.

After the Shabbat service, Hans and the children returned home for lunch. Hans always collapsed after this and had a good sleep. Having had a long, hard week teaching all day at SACS, and then with two evening classes in the university, Hans always enjoyed a good afternoon sleep. 'The best time of the week,' as he used to say.

On Sundays, my mother and aunt came for lunch. I can still see them arriving, wearing smart hats and carrying handbags. In good weather we would go out for a picnic and collect them en route. We would all bring special food. There were many lovely places to visit.

The town of Muizenberg, with a vast, sweeping, sandy beach around False Bay, was close by. We would often swim in the warm waters of the Indian Ocean, or further along at St James, Fishhoek, or the Boulders in Simonstown, a British Naval Base.

Sometimes, we would drive in another direction on the far side of the peninsula on the colder Atlantic Seaboard to a place called Hout Bay, or further on to False Bay or to Strand, where we had glorious swims. Then we would relax in a wooded area, where Hans played a game with the children. He walked around the site to discover which of the many trees was the 'toffee tree', and then we would sit under that tree. As we were having our picnic, sitting on a rug under the trees, suddenly toffees would fall down upon us. This was great fun for the children.

Occasionally, we'd drive into the wooded slopes of Jonkershoek. We were spoilt for choice in the wonderful Western Cape.

Our Friends

As the years progressed, we made many good friends. Our local doctor, Lionel Blumenthal, and his wife Beryl, lived quite close to us. Lionel would recommend the latest Hitchcock film, which Hans would then enjoy seeing. We made many new friends through the Hertzbergs, who we saw very frequently.

My mother and aunt soon reconnected with friends who had come from Liverpool. Mrs Goodman, for one, would give us a delicious tea in her flat in Seapoint. My mother and aunt played bridge with our neighbours, who also came from England. One day, Hans was standing waiting at a bus stop and met Harry Fellstein, who he knew from the Jewish Ex-Service League. 'I'm waiting for my wife's aunt, Miss Reed,' he told Harry.

'My first teacher was a Miss Reed,' said Harry, 'at the Jewish Orphanage' – and with delight he recognised her as she came to meet Hans. After that, Harry and his wife enjoyed visiting my mother and my aunt very frequently. What a small world.

Many years later, Harry invited us to his workshop, called Silvercraft, where he worked as a silversmith with precious metals. He made silverware of all kinds and mended any silver that needed attention. His firm, Silvercraft, was well-known. When the Nationalists came into power and we left the Commonwealth, probably around 1961, the Nationalists did not wish to use any of the British symbols of government. Harry said we should come to his workshop, as he wished to show me something special.

In the corner was an object which was covered with a nondescript cloth. This he took off, revealing a magnificent golden object about three feet in height. It was the new mace for Parliament and had been designed and crafted by Harry himself from the finest South African gold. They little knew, he said, that it was designed and made by a poor Jewish boy from the East End of London.

My special friends Cynthia and Abe Adelstein, from Johannesburg and Pretoria, came to live in Cape Town. Dr Abe Adelstein had been ill and Cynthia had taken him to America for treatment. They settled in Wynberg, which was nearby.

My good friend Margaret Tasman, who had married Reg Rainey and lived in Kenya (he was in charge of locust control), wrote to tell me that when Reg was away travelling, his youngest daughter Janet fell ill with polio and died before his return home. They came to see us with their two sons, as they had decided to return to England. For the first time, we all went with them on a special trip by cable car to the top of Table Mountain.

Chapter Twenty-Four.

SPECIAL EVENTS. BERGVLIET

When the children were little, birthdays were something special. When David's friends came for his celebration, on 30th January, it was summer time and the boys enjoyed playing cricket. I remember how at this age they all had very healthy appetites. We built a barbecue made of bricks, called in South Africa a 'braaivlei' (Afrikaans word), and the boys devoured the chops which we cooked over the fire; and, no sooner had they eaten one chop and sausage, but they were in line for some more.

When Erica had her birthdays on 16th July, it was winter time and we made our own entertainment. Before I came to South Africa, when I was working as a teacher in England, I attended a one-day course run by puppeteers and bought a number of the puppets that they had made themselves. Later, when teaching in Pretoria, I ordered a few more. I also sent away for the plans for how to build a puppet theatre. I had this puppet theatre built when I was living in Pretoria. It was about a yard long, with a curtain that was pulled in front and a backcloth. It would stand on a table and we would sit behind, resting our elbows on the table, with the glove puppets on our hands and fingers. The children loved these performances, and Hans gave very dramatic performances when working the glove puppets.

We made up plays. I remember one story about a cat who stole a fish, which Hans liked to tell in English and Afrikaans.

The little black cat puppet would move in cat-like fashion, sniffing with its long whiskers and saying in Afrikaans, 'Wat ryk so lekker hier?' This translates as, 'What smells so delicious here?'

I remember particularly a story where the witch waved her wand over a puppet rabbit and with great flourish Hans would say, '*Abracadabrakadar*', and our real rabbit (from the back garden) dramatically appeared as if by magic. The children gasped, clapped and laughed. Our puppet shows were a great success.

Our Trip to the Game Reserve and other events

It was not long after this that we went on a family holiday to the Kruger National Park.

Hans drove all the way through the beautiful Cape mountains and through the Karoo, which is semi-desert. We drove at night so as to avoid the heat of the day. It was a long journey to reach Pretoria, before going through the Northern Transvaal to the Kruger National Park (in Gauteng province).

Our car was so laden with luggage, and we travelled so slowly, that every car seemed to overtake us. But it was a great experience. In those days, the Game Reserve was relatively unspoilt. As we drove along, we were fortunate enough to catch sight of deer, impala, warthogs, zebra, and very often we saw prides of lions, herds of elephants and giraffes eating the leaves from tall trees.

We were informed that it was safe to get close up to these animals in your motor-car, but you were forbidden to get out of the car, as this would have been foolhardy and dangerous. Tourists stayed in restricted areas. We did not go to the extreme north of this vast reserve, which ended on the border of Mozambique.

Chapter Twenty-Four. Special Events. Bergvliet

For the first few nights, we stayed in a centre called Skukusa. At night we slept in a large rondavel. These were circular single-roomed homes made of local material, with oval or round thatched roofs. They kept one cool in the hot weather. Early in the morning, before it was light, we heard an African calling, 'Coffee, lekker coffee … warm coffee.'

We dashed out in our dressing gowns to buy the coffee, and after enjoying a hot drink, we set out whilst it was still dark. You might see a lion eating its kill and occasionally an elephant and giraffes and herds of buck. In the evening, you returned to the centre to cook a meal over an open fire. This was a simple affair and very satisfying. That was a winter holiday, as it would be too hot in the summer for such a visit.

Another time during the summer, we drove along the famous Garden Route as far as Knysna. On the way, we stopped at Albertinia, to stay in a very remarkable hotel. We chose this hotel because it offered the most unusual breakfast menu we had ever seen, this included at least twenty items, and you could eat whatever you wished. Hans had a feast: eggs, kippers, haddock and many other irresistible dishes. We continued our journey to Knysna, staying the night in a permanent campsite because we wanted the children to have some experience of taking part in domestic chores such as washing-up the dishes and cooking.

Three interesting events happened in Knysna, which I shall never forget. Knysna is near the great Tsisikama forest, famous for the wood from the trees that are made into furniture. We dressed in simple khaki clothes, suitable for camping. Hans, at the last minute, fished out some of his old army shorts and shirts, which were worn, shabby and really in need of repair. One of the pockets was torn and hanging down, and his whole outfit looked as if it needed repair. Then, with Hans dressed in such a battered old uniform, we were walking along Knysna Lagoon road and who should we see but a tall, distinguished man. Hans recognised him immediately as Brigadier Armstrong. This was the man who had been in charge of the very division in which Hans had been stationed up north. They both recognised each other. Hans was so embarrassed by his clothes, because he thought that Brigadier Armstrong would have thought, 'Poor fellow, there he is with a young family and only his old army uniform to wear. He must really be down on his luck.' They both walked past each other, without speaking.

The holiday went well. We swam every day, but I don't think the children enjoyed the chores, as Hans set up a routine as if they were Army recruits following orders to keep the campsite spick and span. Hans expected them to pick up every tiny piece of paper and keep the floor well swept.

One day, a marionette troupe came to perform nearby. They came from the Afrikaans University of Stellenbosch and were very skilled performers and a delight to watch. Most of their plays were spoken in Afrikaans. In the evening, we went a second time because we had enjoyed it so much. I think they switched to English on our account. A third outing, which we all remember, was taking a small boat up the Knysna river into the wild, natural and unspoilt forest. On the way, we saw a large monkey sitting in the trees, eating a banana.

Chapter Twenty-Five.

DAVID'S BARMITZVAH.
JANUARY 1955

David was now attending the senior school at Wynberg Boys' High, and at the age of thirteen he was about to celebrate his Barmitzvah.

We were in the Great Synagogue attending the Barmitzvah of one of his friends when I noticed he had left the shul. I went out and said to him, 'David, if you can't stay to listen to the service, you certainly can't go to the party afterwards.'

He said, 'I don't want to go to the party. I don't feel well.' He was rushed to hospital and only just avoided a burst appendix. This was an anxious times for me and Hans.

David's barmitzvah service was to be held at Temple Israel, Greenpoint, with Rabbi Sherman. His portion was centred around the Exodus, and Hans taught him his Parsha and the service.

My aunt and uncle and cousin Marcus were planning to come out to enjoy this important family event, but at the last minute my aunt just couldn't face the packing. She was a good age, probably about eighty.

In those days, there were no long-distance aeroplanes as we know them today. Marcus came – wonder of wonders! – by a seaplane instead of the usual long way by ship. This was a new means of transport. It was an amphibious aircraft which could land on sea or land. Quite revolutionary, actually. The journey took seven days, with various stops and changes en route.

After the barmitzvah service in the Reform Synagogue in Greenpoint, we returned to our home in Bergvliet, where we enjoyed a pleasant tea party catered by Crafchik, the well-known local kosher caterer. David remembers that, just before his speech, the very large meringue cake fell face down on the floor. It was picked up immediately, but the dog ate all the leftovers from the floor.

The son of the caterer was a former pupil of Hans at SACS. They made a special fuss of us and provided a lovely spread. Marcus brought, amongst other things, a swanie whistle, which we still have today. Marcus stayed with my mother and Aunt Annie in their flat. I remember on the Sunday we hired a car so that we could all go out together.

Our many Good Friends in South Africa

Hans would from time to time give private lessons to refugees who needed to improve their English, and it was through this that we met Goldie and her husband, Mottel, who had a thriving furniture and clothing business. We soon met the whole Lan family and were invited to the many family events.

Sadly, Mottel died two years later and Goldie passed away years after, but I remain a very close friend with their elder daughter Rebecca to this day.

Chapter Twenty-Five. David's Barmitzvah. January 1955

We were good friends with the two doctors, Louis Mervish, a paediatrician, and Issy, a general consultant. They were both very kind towards us and never charged us a penny for any consultations. Issy introduced us to a social group we called the Chaverim. We met alternate Saturday evenings in each other's houses. All the topics chosen were of a Jewish interest. The members were mainly from Europe and spoke a mixture of Yiddish, Hebrew and English.

It was a puzzle to try and make out what they were saying, partly because of the accents and mixture of languages spoken, and also because of the detail in which they explored the topics under discussion. Women were not expected to contribute much in the way of adding their views, but they had a special role: they were expected to provide a generous tea with homemade cakes. It was quite an experience.

We were also good friends with the Rollnicks, Julian and Sonja. He published books of South African interest under 'The African Bookman' and Sonja had short stories published in the *New Yorker*. Another couple we knew were Wolfgang and Anna Simon. He was a clarinettist in the Cape Town orchestra. She was a refugee from Germany. And there were many others.

In January 1951, and almost as soon as we moved to Bergvliet, we bought a secondhand piano. Hans said that no one who is civilised could possibly live without one. I noted in my diary that on 20th January 1951 we held one of the first of our many family musical evenings. I played the piano, but the best accompanist of all was my Aunt Annie. Hans sang with his fine baritone voice. David played his cello and sometimes Hans played the violin, and with the piano it was a nice trio. Even Erica would sing.

We worked hard and had a pleasant social life. The Herzberg were our neighbours and their house backed onto ours, and so we decided to make a style in the fence so that we could climb over easily to see each other. There was much coming backwards and forwards over the fence. Erica was friendly with Wendy Hertzberg and there she had other friends next door: Jeanie and Daphne Millar. Carol Taylor also lived in the same road. David was friendly with the sons of the Schaffers.

Chapter Twenty-Six.

SAD NEWS IN THE FAMILY

About two and a half months before our family holiday to the Kruger National Park, my mother and Aunt Annie and the family were sitting at our table, enjoying our Sunday tea, when the telephone rang. Hans went out to answer it.

'Who was that?' I asked.

'Oh, somebody enquiring if I have booked for the Kruger National Park,' he said. How very strange, we all said, and continued our tea. When my aunt and mother had gone home, and the children were in bed, Hans said to me, 'The telephone call was from England to say that your Daddy Myer has just died.'

Apparently, they were sitting enjoying a game of bridge. He had a very good hand. He put down the cards and died within a minute. He was eighty-five years old. I was shocked, but I knew that I had to go and tell my mother and Auntie Annie immediately. I went to see them straightaway. I could not imagine a world without him; he was very much the head of the family and respected by everybody.

When I came to live at Norwood with my aunt and her husband, he took the place of my missing father. I called him from the very first Daddy Myer, although my aunt still remained Aunt Esther. When I was a little girl, he played and gave me my fairy name 'Mushloona Inkadon'.

As I grew older, he always helped me with my homework, and its thanks to his good teaching that I never had difficulty with arithmetic, geometry and algebra. He always tried to widen my horizons and I remember him telling me about the Dreyfuss case, which was going on at the time.

1966. Athlone Training Centre. Myself with my class of students. South Africa.

Aunt Esther's 100th Birthday Party. Cousin Ruth, Uncle Louis, Aunt Esther, myself.

Israel. Hans and I swimming in the Dead Sea.

Paul Freund, cousin of Hans and I at the Wailing Wall.

Our visit to the Weissenzee Jewish Cemetery in Berlin.

Hans and young Jeremiah saying the Friday night blessing.

One of my favourite pictures of Jeremiah and Esther. 28.2.82.

*Top row: Louisa, myself, Esther,
Below: Jeremiah, Hans, Whiskey, Erica Golders Green. 1996.*

Hans, Jeremiah and Louisa at Drusillas Zoo. Sussex. 1984.

Chapter Twenty-Seven.

HANS VISITS BERLIN FOR THE FIRST TIME AFTER THE WAR

Hans was due a sabbatical leave and in 1956, during his visit to London, he travelled to Berlin, where he was born. This was the first time Hans had returned to his home town in Germany since he left after Kristallnacht in 1938. But, sadly, there was no family there.

When Hans was in Germany and I was in Cape Town, I decided I should join him. David went to stay with our friends, Professor Norman Sapieka, who was Professor of Pharmacology at the University of Cape Town Medical School, and his wife Sim, who had two younger sons and a daughter.

At this time, Erica was due to leave Bergvliet School and start her new school, called Rustenberg Girls' High School. She had not really enjoyed Bergvliet School, and we were glad she was able to move to another school.

Erica went to stay with her best friend in Bergvliet. Her friend, who was eleven, took Erica out on the street trying to pick up a boyfriend, and when our good friend and neighbour Bernard Hertzberg saw her standing on a street corner looking lost and unhappy, he took her to their home. She stayed with Lily and Bernard during the week and at the weekend Erica went to stay with my mother and aunt in Kenilworth.

Hans and I went on an interesting trip whilst we were in London. First, we went to Berlin and then crossed over to East Berlin, which was an adventure via Checkpoint Charlie. Hans brought me to Germany after his previous visit. This experience was quite dramatic, as the wall was still dividing the two Germanys and the Cold War was in place.

We went by train to Usedom, a spa on the Baltic coast, where Hans had spent many holidays when he was young. Here, there was no tide and I remember walking along in the evening, hearing the nightingales singing at dusk.

We visited Greifswald, where Hans had been a student before the war in the early 1930s. He knocked on the door of a house where he had boarded. When the door was opened, the daughter of the house looked at Hans and recognised him immediately and said: 'Hans Freund, come in!'

This was thirty years after Hans had left, during which time the Second World War had taken place. They talked about old times and fellow students. They talked about one of the students, who had been an open Nazi, before Hitler had actually come into power.

While we were in the DDR, there was a young man who seemed to follow us all the time. I suppose he was there to keep an eye on us. He was very pleasant, and Hans asked him to help us to carry our luggage when necessary. When we were in Berlin, Hans took me to Badstrasse 33 in Wedding, to show me the shop where his parents had their business. The family lived above their large shop

Chapter Twenty-Seven. Hans visits Berlin for the first time after the War

and Hans was born there. Hans lived in that flat until the day he left Germany.

We returned to London by coach via Hamburg and Amsterdam. We stayed in the beautiful city of Hamburg. We visited the famous Reeperbahn, with its night-clubs, and this was for me somewhat of an eye opener. We took a boat around the harbour. Later, in Amsterdam, we visited the art galleries, including the Rijks Museum, Rembrandt's House and the famous old synagogue, and then we continued to Paris.

We went to the Folies Bergère and many wonderful art galleries. We visited the palace of Versailles.

We had missed our connection because we couldn't tear ourselves away from the beautiful city of Paris. For this reason, we were forced to go all the way to Le Havre to take the boat across the Channel and back to England. It was a horrendous journey. The train proceeded slowly at night through snow, high winds and a great storm. Instead of arriving in the early evening, we only reached Le Havre in the morning of the next day. There was no provision for food and we had nothing whatsoever to eat during this terrible night. There were no beds and all we could do was to sit upright in our compartment. When we left the train, I went to thank the two drivers of this huge steaming engine, which had a snowplough in front. An unforgettable experience.

At last we embarked, and as we had had no supper and were starving, we had a large, substantial breakfast. Then, when the boat left the harbour, I was very seasick and only just managed to get to my berth and lie down. It didn't seem to upset Hans in the slightest. He said to me, 'Are you all right? Do you want a blanket?' And I was too ill to say 'yes'. What a joy it was to finally arrive in the calm waters of the English Channel and finally reach home in London.

Chapter Twenty-Eight.

FEARS ABOUT THE POLITICAL SITUATION

Although it affected us greatly, I have in this book rarely mentioned the political situation in South Africa. From the beginning of my life in South Africa, I was well aware of inequality in the society and the unfairness shown to Africans and mixed-race people, who made up the majority of the population. While General Smuts was the Prime Minister, there was still hope of improvement to change this unjust situation. The opposing party, the Nationalists, known as the 'Nats', never forgot the Boer War and still held onto much bitterness and dislike of Britain.

It was known that during the Second World War there were many Nationalists who hoped that Germany would win. We felt anxious that the growing strength of the Nationalist Party meant that they could take power. This occurred in 1948 when they won with a very small majority. They defeated General Smuts. Remember that the vast majority of South Africans had no vote at all at this time. Almost as soon as the Nationalist Party came into power, they started to introduce draconian restrictive Acts of Parliament, such as the Mixed Marriages Act and Relations in 1949, which banned marriages between different races, and the Immorality Act was passed in 1950 and 1951. Soon, everyone was given an identity card, which indicated whether you were white, black or 'coloured', with personal details. Every black person was forced to carry a pass. They were restricted in many different ways. The Group Areas Act 1950 forced many people out of their homes and African people back to their tribal homelands.

For example, Cape Town's District Six, a very pleasant area on the side of the mountain looking down onto the port, had previously been an area where people of mixed race lived peaceably side by side with white people. Because of this Act, all the non-white people were made to move into the dry, arid area of the Cape Flats. This affected me in various ways.

I had been teaching at a night school where mixed-race men and women hoped to improve their education and gain some qualifications to better their lives. This work was very rewarding, and I felt it was valuable work, but under the new laws it was completely outlawed, and the school was closed down as the coloured people had to move out of the area in District Six. At our college, we had been helping a very charming 'coloured' lady, by the descriptive name of Mrs Waterwitch, to support a nursery school which she had started and which was flourishing.

She told me sadly how she had been forced to move out to a place on the Cape Flats where she said it was difficult to even grow grass. There was a famous Jewish shop in District Six where you could buy religious books as well as matzahs at Pesach time. It was owned by a Mr Benkinstadt. I believe Mr Mottel Lan's furniture shop was forced to close. As they were slightly outside of the designated boundaries of District Six, they received no compensation whatsoever.

There were Acts passed like the Suppression of Communism, which seemed to us to be acts of a fascist regime. In reality, the country was now a police state, and any ideas that opposed those of the Nationalist Party were made unlawful and seen as crimes against the State. We were living in a violent society, where the rule of law had disappeared. I remember our friends taking all their left-wing books and leaving them outside the university library, because they were afraid of being discovered having those kind of books in their possession. The people of mixed race were soon removed from the voters' roll and three representatives who were white were appointed. The Separate Amenities Act of 1953 affected us all greatly. Separate buses were introduced and separate entrances to all public places. You saw benches in parks with signs saying that 'whites only' could sit on them. It was a very unhappy state of affairs.

These Acts did not go without considerable opposition. I remember marching with ex-servicemen in the early days of this repression to hand in a letter of protest to Parliament. There were other demonstrations and marches against these unfair laws. A group of women called the Black Sash stood outside Parliament to protest at the disgraceful laws that meant forms of protest were suppressed and people were arrested in the middle of the night, dragged off and kept in solitary confinement. Peaceful protest seemed to achieve no change.

As the years passed, we felt increasingly apprehensive and threatened by the political situation and considered that at some stage we might have to leave what had become a country ruled by a fascist regime.

Chapter Twenty-Nine.

THE MOVE TO RONDEBOSCH

In 1956, after Hans and I had returned from our holiday in Europe and London, David made an interesting suggestion. He said that in two years he would be leaving Wynberg Boys' High School and going to the University of Cape Town. Erica was already at Rustenberg School for Girls in Rondebosch. Hans and I were working in this area. 'Wouldn't it be a good idea for us to move nearer to Cape Town and Rondebosch?' David said.

I agreed it was a good plan and put the suggestion to Hans and Erica. We found an estate agent who was prepared to sell our house in Bergvliet and to find accommodation nearer to Cape Town. Quite soon, he found a suitable buyer for our house in Eksteen Avenue, but we were not so fortunate in finding a suitable house to buy. We decided to sell our house and move into a hotel, which I think was called Thornton House Hotel, until we found somewhere permanent. Today, of course, one would not dream of doing this with these rising prices; but in those days it was a sensible plan. We put all our furniture and belongings into storage.

Hans and I had an extremely large room on the first floor and Erica had a bed in the corner. David had a room in an annexe of his own. We all enjoyed this temporary change. It was lovely for me not to have to think about meals, and it was fairly easy for Erica to get to her school. I think David enjoyed being rather more independent.

He had a good neighbour that he always remembers as Colonel Stallard, who was a retired Northern Rhodesian (now Zambia) policeman. He played the double bass and often held musical evenings. He had some very interesting African artefacts that he had confiscated in rural Rhodesia that both Bernard Herzberg and we subsequently bought, such as spears, 'knobkerries' (wooden club) and karimbas (plucking musical instruments), which I still have at home. David was able to walk to school. He continued to have his lunches at my mother's flat with Aunt Annie. His lunch was always followed by the usual two sweets. Arnold Lorie, David's previous Junior Headmaster, lent him the key of the school so that he could practise the cello there.

For three months we looked at different properties and at last we found a delightful house in Rondebosch. It was situated on the mountain side of the Main Road and was on Highstead Road. The house was named 'Dulton'. We remained a further two weeks in the hotel while alterations were carried out in the house we had bought.

Eventually, in 1957, we moved even before these minor alterations were finished. Highstead Road was a short road, built along the lower slopes of Table Mountain, with green trees on either side. There were a few small blocks of flats opposite, but everything was moderately sized. The house was designed by a Dutch architect who had lived in it for a time. It had a steep roof with attractive tiles, a garage and a front door which, when we removed the white paint, was made of solid oak.

Inside was a very large, interestingly shaped lounge, a small dining room, and another room that looked out onto the road. It had a built-in hall cupboard, a downstairs bathroom and lavatory, a rather dark kitchen, and servants' accommodation close to the kitchen. Best of all was a large sheltered stoep or veranda, where we spent most of our time and meals, looking over a well-designed and

Chapter Twenty-Nine. The move to Rondebosch

attractive garden. On the ground floor was a large bedroom for David. The wide wooden staircase led up to the first floor, where there was a landing and a spacious bedroom for us, a bedroom for Erica, and a large bathroom. There was a third bed- room with an interconnecting smaller room, equipped as a little kitchen, with its own entrance from the second-floor veranda that could be reached by an outside staircase.

We decided to let this as separate accommodation, which would be a welcome source of income, and over the years we had a variety of interesting tenants.

At the top of our road was a small wood, and walking through the trees we came to the extensive and beautiful grounds of a majestic house called Groote Schuur. Groote Schuur was, at the time, the official residence of the Prime Minister. It was a very grand building, surrounded by areas of well-kept ornamental gardens. Further up the slopes of Table Mountain were pine trees which led up to the small zoo and Cape Town University. At night you could hear the lions roar.

Miss Allen, the senior English teacher at Erica's school, lived opposite, and we often went on early evening walks together. In those days you could walk through the Prime Minister's grounds. There were security police guarding the grounds, but we were allowed to walk about in the nearby woods.

After a year, the Schaffers moved into a flat next door. It was really lovely to have our good friends Walt and Gladys nearby. In the flats opposite lived an English Jewish tailor, and he made a suit for Hans from material that I had bought on a visit to London. Erica went to school by bicycle, crossing over the main road and the railway line. When David started studying at Cape Town University, he could walk through the woods, then up the steep road that led up the mountain to the university. I went to the next station, which was Rondebosch, to Berkeley House and Hans took the car to the school where he was teaching (SACS). Sometimes he would pick me up. It was all very convenient.

Chapter Thirty.

LIFE CHANGES

Despite the growing feeling of insecurity with our worry about the political situation, our move to Rondebosch was worthwhile. We were not far from the centre of Cape Town and could enjoy the concerts at the City Hall and visit the Little Theatre, as well as being able to go to other venues. We enjoyed attending symphony and popular Sunday concerts.

We went to listen to a lecture by Ze'ev Jabotinsky, a well-known Zionist who had lately come from Israel.

Over the years we made many new friends, some of whom lectured at the university. One couple was Philip Segal and his wife Gerda. He was a senior lecturer in English, becoming Professor at Witwatersrand University in Johannesburg. Gerda worked for a fine household store of beautifully designed items for the home. Wolfgang Simon was a clarinettist in the Cape Town Orchestra.

Evelyn Hutchinson taught David the cello. She sold us our first Cairn terrier, Shauna, 'Muck of the Lake was her pedigree name. Sadly, David's cello teacher Evelyn Hutchinson died two years before David's matric year and a good friend Mr Arnold Lorie, the Junior School Headmaster at Wynberg Junior School, organised Granville Britton the first cellist in the Cape Town City Orchestra, to teach David through Matric.

Many important personalities came to Cape Town, such as Sophie Tucker, and several well-known conductors would stay for our winter season, which was summertime in the northern hemisphere. These included Sir Anthony Collins, Sir Charles Grove and the great composer Stravinsky on a world tour.

There were summer schools at the university which were open to young and old, and David and Erica enjoyed these courses very much. David went to hear a talk by Chief Albert Lutuli, who had recently come out of jail and who, before Nelson Mandela, was the chief spokesman for the African people. David said he would never forget the experience. He was the only white person in Rondebosch Town Hall. The hall was packed.

During these years, David passed his school examinations and started studying in the School of Architecture at the university. Erica was quite settled in her school and made many good friends. In short, although times were difficult, we had a happy social life.

I was still working at the Berkeley House Training College for Nursery Education and at some stage had left the Buxton Demonstration School and was now in charge of one of the two Berkeley House Nursery schools at Berkeley House. I also taught the students attending the Buxton Training College general education and was responsible for the training of students in the nursery school. My speciality was the art of storytelling and choosing suitable books and literature for preschool children. Together with my friend Sim Sapeika, I had started an enjoyable class of four or five friends learning to improve our dressmaking skills. Magda Sprenger, the wife of the manager of the Cape Town branch of Barclays Bank, was our instructor. I made clothes, using Vogue or Butterick patterns, that were of a professional standard, for myself and Erica. It was a lovely group of women. Magda gave us delicious teas at her house during the class.

Chapter Thirty. Life Changes

My mother and Auntie Annie decided they would return to London. There were many farewells and especially a nice present for Auntie Annie both at the Reform Hebrew School and at the South African College, where she had always been much appreciated as accompanist. They gave up their flat and returned to England on a Union Castle liner. I was very sorry to see them leave. Hardly had they arrived in England, when I got a telegram to say that they were coming back, and could I book them another flat. I tried to get their old flat back. This was not possible, but fortunately there was another flat vacant, which was even nicer. They found life in London very different and probably couldn't cope with the change. So, happily, they returned. But I don't think they gave back the presents that had been given to them on their farewell!

News about Germany reaches us

As far as the news was concerned, remember there was no television, although we were able to hear the BBC World Service and enjoyed many wonderful programmes, such as 'Much Binding in the Marsh'. Partly for this reason we went quite frequently to the cinema to watch the Gaumont British News.

We were able to get less-biased and more honest news from a paper called *The Guardian*, edited by Lionel Foreman. The Government banned and shut down this paper from time to time, but it continued to re-open under a new title.

Incidentally, it was only on the news that we first heard of the terrible deaths of thousands of our Jewish compatriots in Auschwitz and Belsen. My cousin Marcus, who was then a Wing Commander with Field Marshal Montgomery, entered Belsen on the first day of its liberation. Although he didn't talk about it, I still have some small photographs that he took of this terrible place.

One Saturday morning, Erica came rushing into our room to tell us that the Prime Minister Henrik Verwoerd had been shot and was in a very serious condition. This was followed by the most gloomy, solemn music, but as he improved it became less serious. It was six years later that we learnt a white man had finally assassinated him. The assassin was a tenant living in the house of one of our friends, the Shulmans, who lived nearby. Mr Shulman played the organ at Temple Israel and my mother and aunt often played bridge with him.

Around this time, on 21 March 1960, we were shocked to hear how the police had fired on and killed Africans at a township outside Johannesburg called Sharpeville. The people of Sharpeville were staging a peaceful protest against the pass laws and the apartheid laws. We were shocked and all our friends were discussing this. Hans said that he did not want to live his life in another fascist country and I suggested we consider returning to England. Hans thought he would wait until he could collect his pension when he was fifty-five. That would be 1965. Another five years and then we would emigrate to the UK.

My work at Athlone Training Centre

In 1963, I did not return to work at Berkeley House as I felt I needed a break after working for so many years. Shortly afterwards, I was offered an interesting post establishing a new training course at a centre for mixed-race students, what we then called 'coloured' students. Education in South Africa was segregated, and this meant that my work came under the Department of Coloured Affairs. The aim of the course was to train suitable candidates to become nursery-school teachers for mixed-race children in schools. There were already some schools, but they lacked trained staff. The course was first established by the efforts of the white parents of the children that attended the Berkeley House schools.

Chapter Thirty. Life Changes

Attending the course were about twenty-five women students of varying ages. One was a grandmother. The training course was held at the Coloured Nursery School in Athlone. I shared an office with a splendid woman, who was in charge of the nursery school.

She held very liberal views and was a member of the Black Sash, which I have already described. This was the most interesting post that I had ever had, and I enjoyed organising the curriculum. I taught the aims of the Nursery School Movement, the methods and something of its recent history. Mrs Myberg, herself of mixed race and a teacher in a school, taught the students Afrikaans. Then members of the Berkeley House staff came to teach the students toy-making and how to make and mend suitable nursery-school equipment. In addition, I also taught them the art of storytelling and included introducing them to many suitable nursery songs with finger plays. A nurse from Berkeley House came to teach them about health.

The students were wary of me at first, as probably they had not had a white teacher before in this very socially divided country. But gradually a good relationship was built up between us. Part of my duty was to find them suitable work-place experience. This was not easy, because at that time there were so few schools catering for the younger child. The course lasted for eighteen months.

They started their work experience by two students at a time carrying out careful observations in different nursery schools such as Berkeley House and the Buxton Nursery School.

There was a school in the country at some distance from Cape Town, in Elgin, an apple farm. There were two schools at the Athlone Centre: *Cafda*, a large welfare organisation that had a school, and another centre near Muizenberg. I wanted them to see the development of a baby before the child was old enough to attend nursery school. They went to observe at a maternity home.

Mrs Waterwitch, who was running her own private nursery school, was pleased to take two students at a time to observe and work in her nursery. She was a woman of mixed race, very enterprising and brave, who had worked hard despite compulsory eviction from her home in District Six and being moved to the Cape Flats. She then re-established her school, which answered a great need in the area.

When the course drew to an end, it was my responsibility to recruit new students for the next training course, and I had to write to many institutions in South Africa to gather suitable applicants. In the second course, three nuns from Natal, as well as students from quite distant places, came to register for the course.

When I retired from the course, the students showed great appreciation of the work we had done together. We held an exhibition at the end of the course, showing some of the toys they had made, and each student made a book with songs and stories illustrating their work. Everyone who came to see the exhibition was highly impressed. One of the students painted an attractive watercolour of the Cape, and all the students signed their names. To this day I have the painting hanging on my wall.

In 1966, when the time came for me to leave South Africa, I was to leave this work, but was confident that it was now well established.

Chapter Thirty-One.

ILLNESS IN THE FAMILY. AUNTIE ANNIE

Before this, in 1959 or 1960, my dear Aunt Annie contracted a vehement form of cancer. Ten years previously, she did have a breast operation, but had recovered and enjoyed good health until the second illness set in. She went into Groote Schuur Hospital, and her surgeon was Dr Hesselson. I knew him well, as his daughter had been a little pupil at my nursery school. He gave her pills, but we realised that it could not be cured. She wanted to come home, and my mother agreed willingly.

Throughout this time, my mother behaved very bravely and courageously. I remember that I took Aunt Annie home by car and when she saw the busy roads she exclaimed: 'Here are all these people going around their business as usual.'

Once we had brought her home, she was confined to her bed and we employed a nurse to care for her. I remember Erica and her friend Hilary Milner came and sang to her some of her favourite songs. Aunt Annie loved music throughout her life and was a very gifted pianist. She said to me, 'If I lie perfectly still, I'm not in pain.' But eventually she drifted into a coma. I was sitting next to her at this stage, when she suddenly opened her eyes and said to me, 'Have I had a stroke?' I was about to answer her, when she said, 'Listen to me', and passed away. This was the first time that I had experienced the loss of a loved one.

She looked very peaceful. My mother employed a 'watcher' beside her bed, which is a Jewish custom. She was cremated soon after. My mother kept her ashes and eventually took them back to be placed in the Jewish Crematorium in Golders Green. We all missed her very much, with her sweet smile and her loving ways. My mother returned to England after Annie's death and stayed first in London with Esther and Marcus and then in Liverpool with my Aunt Clara.

Our move to England

Our life in Rondesbosch continued. David did well at his music and gained a distinction pass, despite being taught the wrong syllabus. He also won the award for the best instrumental player in the Cape Town Eisteddfod. In 1961, Erica passed her matric with a first-class pass and distinctions in French, and to everyone's amazement also in Geography. I believe the Geography teacher couldn't believe it. That was because, according to Erica, she had often talked in class and had missed many lessons when the teacher had made her stand outside the door. But her distinctions were merited. After this, Erica went to university to study Social Science. I did not realise how distressing the practical side would be in apartheid South Africa. And many of the things that she saw and had to do were grim.

Once South Africa was no longer in the Commonwealth, the UK gave South Africans five years in which to decide whether they wished to remain British or lose this right. Hans was able to retire in 1965 at the age of fifty-five. The family came to a big decision, and both Hans and Erica left for England, where they applied for British citizenship. Erica was glad to abandon her Social Studies university degree.

In England, she wanted to study Drama as a subject and went to Furzedown Teacher Training College, where I had studied many years before. Erica trained as a teacher with Drama as her main subject. While Hans and Erica were away in England, I managed to sell the house and started to dispose of the articles and furniture that we did not want to take with us to England. I remember that I put many articles in one room and invited my friends to take something as a friendly memento. Meanwhile, David, who had returned from his Architectural Studies in England, was now studying at the Art College in Cape Town. He won the South African Prize for Art, which entitled him to study in Germany. When Hans returned to South Africa, I left for England, leaving Hans to dispose of what remained of our furniture.

We were glad to leave South Africa with its racist, fascist government, but sorry to say goodbye to our friends and the beautiful Cape. Many of our friends were also preparing to emigrate. Mallie and Walter Katz had already left for London. Graham Watson had gone to Canada. We left David in Cape Town to await the time for when he would go to Berlin. When Hans came to London, he stayed with his cousins the Rubens and I stayed with Auntie Esther in Palace Gate. It was difficult to find any suitable accommodation. Eventually, Hans's relations, Rosie and Lily, who worked for the BBC, heard of somebody who was leaving their rented flat in Cleveland Square, Bayswater. This was on the top floor of a converted Regency house, with a small lift that took us up to our fourth floor. We had to pay the present occupant key money and we could take over her lease of the flat.

There was one sitting room, one bedroom and a small second bedroom, as well as a tiny kitchen. The flat overlooked the square and was in a very pleasant position. Erica stayed in the little room until she went to live closer to Furzedown College. Before Hans came, I bought a car for us from the garage that Marcus partly owned. The garage was called Peregrine Garage. Hans had obtained a teaching post in Feltham, in a comprehensive school. This was some distance from where we lived, and each weekday he drove there and back.

Summer 2019. Our Garden in Golders Green.

Hans and I on holiday walking along Regent's Street, London.

2019. Good friends visit. left to right: Malcolm, Becky Sacks, myself, David, Gaby Marks and Leah.

Erica's children: Louisa, Jeremiah and Esther, all three of my grandchildren together.

David playing The Macello Sonata.

My daughter Erica aged 3 years.

Chapter Thirty-Two.

OUR NEW HOME IN GOLDERS GREEN

Meanwhile, I tried to find a house that we could buy, as this flat was not for sale. I found quite an attractive house near Kew Gardens, but at the last minute I thought, 'I don't know a soul here. It's not for me.' Then my mother found part of a house in Westbourne Terrace, near to Kensington Gardens. It was in a very good position and would have been near the relations, but David and Erica didn't like it. They said it was not a proper home. At length, my friend Cynthia Adelstein rang me to say there was a house for sale near to where she was living in Golders Green. I came out and visited number 13 Dunstan Road and thought it was both attractive and very suitable. It had five bedrooms, a dining room and a lounge and a kitchen, a front garden and a pleasant back garden.

Cynthia and I walked to the nearby Golders Hill Park, and when I saw the lake, the trees and Hampstead Heath beyond, I made up my mind the house would suit us. When Hans came, he looked at it and agreed that it was fine. Before we moved in, we made a few alterations, spending as much as we could afford. In the place of the scullery we put in a downstairs bathroom and toilet, we modernised the kitchen and had most of the rooms painted the colour magnolia.

The house cost seven thousand pounds and in addition we took out a mortgage. I think our mortgage was four thousand pounds. In 1968, after some weeks when the alterations were carried out, we moved in. I still wish we could have bought the little flat in Cleveland Square, but that wasn't possible. For the first time we did not have a garage and the car had to be parked outside the front door. However, we discovered that the attic could be doubled in size, and that was very useful indeed. It has always been packed full to this day. All of our furniture from South Africa could now be delivered. And we bought some additional, necessary furniture.

Our house in Golders Green was in a part of London not well known to me at the time, though when I was growing up and living in Norwood I had visited my Uncle Louis, who lived in a house in Wessex Gardens in this part of North London.

However, I soon made friends with my new neighbours in Dunstan Road. It was a pleasure to have our friends, the Adelsteins, living in the same road.

We had a number of friends from South Africa living nearby. So many of our friends had left South Africa because they were unhappy about living under the apartheid government. Directly opposite our house in Dunstan Road live a family of ultra-orthodox Jews. We see them spend their time visiting a Shtetel in the neighbouring road. On our side of the road lived many friends, such as the Ackermans from South Africa. Ken worked for the BBC as a chief lighting engineer. His wife Joan's father was our solicitor in Cape Town. Number 9 was divided into two flats. The Jacobsons lived upstairs. They both came from South Africa. Ruth came from Johannesburg. She was a remarkable woman. She devoted her time to helping handicapped people. Much later, when I became partially sighted, she would come and read to me each week. Next door to me at number 15 lived an interesting old lady from Germany. She had worked at the Tavistock Clinic for many years.

Next door to her lived the Simms. Her name constantly appeared in letters to the *Guardian* regarding women's rights. I made great friends with Dorothy Brown and her husband. Dorothy worked for ITV and her husband was a psycho-therapist. Next door to Abe and Cynthia lived an old friend, Ken Dixon, who we knew from Cape Town. When we had worked at the Cape Town Jewish Orphanage, Ken had been one of the senior boys. He had become an architect and it gave him great pleasure to redesign parts of our house.

Quite soon after we moved in, Ken Ackerman organised a Residents' Association. We arranged for a barrier to be installed which narrowed the road to prevent the large vehicles from hurtling down Dunstan Road. For many years I was the treasurer, collecting all the fees and subscriptions. We held our Annual General Meetings in the Dunstan Road Synagogue Hall. Over the course of several years, we all got to know one another and held street parties to celebrate important occasions. Very soon we made many friends and soon settled down in Britain.

David completed his studies in Germany and joined us in England. He worked for some time for the BBC in television and later Erica took a post teaching in Lambeth, Newington Butts.

Life continued in a new country with both old and new friends.

My work as a lecturer at Maria Grey College

A few months after we had moved in, I was offered a post at the Maria Grey College of Education in Isleworth. The college was housed in a large, attractive building on the banks of the Thames.

I was told the post would be offered to me at the end of a year and I decided to take a course at the London School of Education, just to bring me up to date with the new educational methods. When I was due to start the course, I developed a painful backache – probably psychological – and I landed up in hospital for a few days and decided not to undertake the course.

In the summer before I was due to start my new post, I asked my superior, Mary Presland, what I should prepare, and she said do something about Freud. Maybe that was because my name was Freund. This took up all my time during my summer holiday, preparing details about this famous man – as, in truth, I knew very little about the psychologist Sigmund Freud!

David managed to find a secondhand motor-car, a Rover 110, with its original radio, walnut dashboard and leather seats. I drove quite near to the school in Feltham where Hans was teaching, but I needed a car because my timetable was different to his. I was responsible for one of the four groups of mature students who were taking, over a period of three years, a two-year teacher training course.

The students were able to bring their children to a nursery school in the grounds on the two or three afternoons when they came to study. I had no idea that there would be so much theory of education in the syllabus. To be quite honest, as far as this side of the programme was concerned, I had no inkling at all. I knew little more than the students.

For example, the theories of Piaget were unknown to me. Hans was very helpful and would type out pages of suitable books, none of which I had read myself. When the students went on school practice it was different, and then my practical experience was useful to them.

Chapter Thirty-Two. Our new home in Golders Green

I visited the schools all over west and north London, where my students were doing their practice teaching. I had to study the map carefully to find how to get to some of these unknown places. Soon, the college expanded, and more lecturers were employed.

A large new building was erected and there followed heated discussions as to choosing a suitable name. Finally, my friend and lecturer in education, Ann Smith, said, 'Why don't we call it after the original owner of the site?' His name was Moses Hart. And this was agreed. I later discovered that Moses Hart had been a well-known Jewish financier in the 19th century. In those days one of the easiest ways to get to the city was by boat, and this surely must have been convenient.

At the college I made several good friends. Lecturers were very helpful and co-operative. I enjoyed these visits to the various schools. When I turned sixty, I retired, but was asked to continue to help students on school practice for some time after that. With retirement, I had to adapt myself to another stage of life.

Chapter Thirty-Three.

OUR LIFE IN ENGLAND

We join the B'nai B'rith

When we lived in Cape Town, Hans had joined a branch of the B'nai B'rith. This is a worldwide Jewish charitable and social organisation. After our settling in London, Hans had to choose to become a member of either the First Lodge or the Leo Baeck Lodge.

The chairman of First Lodge had a hotel overlooking Kensington Gardens, right near to our hotel. He was delighted to enrol Hans and take him to the meetings. I went with them occasionally.

I did not join the organisation at that time. As time passed, we tended to go more frequently to the Leo Baeck Lodge. Hans felt more at home there, as the members of this lodge were almost entirely composed of refugees from Nazi Europe. One day, a very interesting member called Frank Falk said to Hans, 'You're coming here very often; why don't you join us?' Hans decided that this was a good idea, and so he became a member of both Lodges. Leo Baeck was a famous German Jewish rabbi who had supported Jewish people in the difficult times in Germany and eventually came himself to London. I remember one day my uncle (Daddy Myer) had introduced me to Leo Baeck when he attended Berkeley Street Synagogue. Hans's two uncles, who were rabbis, had known Leo Baeck in Berlin and attended his study sessions.

Chapter Thirty-Three. Our Life in England

On my retirement, I decided to join the Leo Baeck Lodge. I was enrolled with due ceremony and joined Hans on his weekly visit. Quite soon after enrolling, the Lodge moved to their own building in Fitzjohns Avenue. It provided small flats for people in need, and we had large reception rooms at the rear of this large house. When I joined, the men and women were quite separate and there were at least four hundred women, although they did not always attend. Usually, we would have a lecture together and then separate if there was any business to discuss. All the members had been refugees, and as far as I could make out only one other member, Cissie Powell, had been born in England.

The Powells made us very welcome and invited us to their house by the river, not far from the college where I used to work. Gradually, I met more people in the B'nai B'rith Lodge, and after some time I was asked to be Chairman of the Cultural Activities Committee. My duties were to arrange the programmes, and this helped me to form even more close friendships.

When someone was first admitted as a member of this lodge, it was customary to describe their past history. I found the life stories of how people were forced to leave their homes in Germany most distressing. I thought that there should be a historical record of their heart-breaking experiences. The Committee agreed to my idea.

With the help of three or four other women members, we formed a small sub-committee to carry out this idea. The plan took considerable time. Volunteers who told their story were interviewed individually. Whatever they said was recorded on a special tape and later this was transcribed. There were 73 personal histories of the women, and these have been placed in the Wiener Library, which specialises in the history of the Holocaust. Now, in 2017, after a grant was given to the Wiener Library by our Lodge, they promised to digitalise them and make them available on the internet. This has not yet been done, but I sincerely hope this promise will be carried out.

I think this is a very important project, as now most of these members have passed away. But their stories will remain for others to read and it is important that all they endured should never be forgotten. At this time, the B'nai B'rith was a very active organisation. The Lodge provided many charitable works and also supported members of the Lodge socially and, if need be, by helping members in all sorts of difficulties. Not only did we meet once a week, but there were local groups who met monthly in our homes.

I belonged to the Golders Green Group. Over the years, I became a member of the Israel Committee, Secretary of the Council and, finally, President of the Women's Lodge. Gradually, as the years passed, our numbers decreased and, rather reluctantly, we joined forces with the men.

In 2018, our numbers diminished to such an extent that a decision was taken to close our Lodge and sell the building in Fitzjohns Avenue. It is a sad point that the younger generation showed little interest in continuing our work, and I believe this is true of many Jewish organisations today. I could describe many of our members who were quite remarkable, and this organisation enriched my retirement years in many ways.

Meeting Friends and Family

Besides spending considerable time with Lodge activities, we joined the Alyth Gardens North West London Reform Synagogue, as it was more convenient than Upper Berkeley Street. I had intended to take a more active part in this shul, but somehow the Leo Baeck seemed to take up more of my time.

Shortly after our return to England, I met up with my old Norwood school-friend Rosalind, now married to Arli Kite. She told me that there was now an active Norwood Old Scholars Association. 'Come to one of our committee meetings,' she said. This was a large committee and I knew a majority of the members. At that time, they successfully arranged large balls, partly as fundraisers and partly for pleasure.

After some time, I became President of this Association. We met regularly and sent out a newsletter. This went to all parts of the world where Old Scholars lived. I edited this newsletter and we enlarged it with articles written by many former Norwood Old Scholars. I was responsible for editing the magazine for about eight years. I am now the Honourable Vice-President.

On a Friday evening, we usually went to my Aunt Esther in Palace Gate, Kensington, for Friday night dinner. My cousins Harold and George very often came. My dear Marcus was there, of course. He lived there with his mother. And time passed.

Later, as my Aunt Esther needed more nursing care, she was admitted to a Kensington Hospital, in a ward for the elderly. Marcus visited her every day, but when he was otherwise engaged I would visit her instead. And this was at least once a week. My mother was living with my Aunt Clara in West Kirby, in Cheshire. I travelled by train to Liverpool, and then took another train, which went under the Mersey. This brought me to the pleasant coastal village of West Kirby. In former times and before the tunnel was built, you would go by boat, the HMS *Daffodil*. Every few weeks, I would go to visit her for the weekend.

My Aunt Clara's house was on the Wirral, by the sea. I have happy memories of holidays at West Kirby when I was a child. There is a small island off the coast and at low tide it is easy to walk there.

AS TIME GOES BY

Once, when I was visiting, I walked to the island. On my return, the tide came in quickly and it took me all my strength to get back safely. I didn't tell my mother.

Chapter Thirty-Four.

HOLIDAYS AND TRIPS

My first trip to Israel

In 1959, Marcus wrote and suggested I visit them over the Christmas holidays, and he was prepared to treat me to the ticket. I remember that I decided to apply for a South African passport. I had to be interviewed by a member of the South African police force before I could obtain the passport. The policeman asked me what newspaper I read, and I said *Huisgenoot*, which is a weekly family magazine, something very harmless and non-political. This satisfied his enquiry.

Travelling by air to Israel, we had to go on a roundabout way because South African planes were banned from crossing certain territories in Africa. The journey gave me the opportunity to stop at various places en route and I was able to visit Israel for the first time. Hans's relations met me at the airport and took me to stay with them in Givatayim, which is outside Tel Aviv. Hans's cousin Lotta and her husband were very hospitable. They had a small three-roomed flat; the parents' bedroom converted into the sitting room during the day and I shared a room with their younger son, who was ten years old. After a week, I went to stay with Hans's other cousin Heinie and his wife. I made a trip by bus by myself to Jerusalem to meet two people I had made friends with on the aeroplane. Everyone was extremely friendly, and they took me on a tour round Jerusalem.

AS TIME GOES BY

After that, I flew to Rome for a few days, where I made some interesting tours and then continued on my journey to London, where I stayed at Palace Gate with Marcus and Auntie Esther. After about a fortnight, I returned home to South Africa.

On two other occasions, Hans and I went together to Israel and stayed first in a hotel in Tel Aviv and later with Paul Freund, Hans's cousin in Jerusalem. One night, we suddenly saw the light swinging violently from left to right in our bedroom. It turned out to be part of an earthquake that had occurred not too far away. Hans had far more relations in Israel than I had, and they were very happy indeed to meet him. It gave us both great pleasure to be in the land of Israel among fellow Jews.

Over the years, we made several trips to Berlin. We went when the wall dividing East and West Berlin was still in place and, because we wished to visit the Weissensee Cemetery, in East Berlin, where Hans's parents were buried, we had to go through quite an extensive examination. The people in charge were so helpful.

The Weissensee Cemetery is the largest Jewish cemetery in Europe, and Hans's grandfather had for many years been the Director. We have a life-size painted portrait of his grandfather, which hangs to this day in our sitting room. We were given the opportunity to enter the room and we saw the very chair and the window depicted in the painting. Many of the graves were in need of repair and so we paid for this to be done to our family graves.

In 1981, we visited Moscow. I remember we went to see a large and very beautiful shul. While I was visiting all the various places, Hans spent most of the time with the choir of the shul, learning the Hebrew songs that were sung in Russia as opposed to those that came from Germany. The songs were composed by Lewandowsky. After the service, the choir invited us to a Kiddush. Some members invited us to their country places, which are called dachas. Here they enjoy the country air and many grow fruit and vegetables.

We travelled by train to St Petersburg, passing through many forests and beautiful countryside. St Petersburg is an attractive city, said to be comparable to Venice. We visited a large cemetery, where many hundreds of Russian people were buried in mass graves. These were the people who died mainly from starvation after having been surrounded by the German army during the Second World War. This was a very moving experience for both of us.

We visited a large square close to a harbour, where the famous battleship *Potemkin* is permanently stationed. It is a reminder that the revolution against the Tsar started on this famous ship. To reach the harbour, you have to descend many wide and dramatic steps. We watched a school party of children going down to see the boat. It was noticeable in St Petersburg that, although people were dressed very plainly, the children were obviously specially dressed by loving parents.

In 1988, we had a very special holiday. We flew to Calgary in Canada, where our friends the Watsons had a beautiful house by the river. Then, after a few days, we took the train for a night and a day to reach Vancouver, passing through beautiful forests and rivers and seeing otters and beavers, all a very remarkable sight. We were able to sit in the observation coach. This was a better way to see the scenery. Hans, of course, sang and played his mouth organ, and everyone enjoyed a feeling of camaraderie.

Vancouver is a remarkably beautiful city, surrounded by mountains. Not unlike Cape Town, but perhaps even grander. We then took a boat to Vancouver Island, an indescribably beautiful journey. We stayed with friends of the Watsons who had many children, including a West Indian adopted son. They were most hospitable, but ate rather less than we needed, and so we had to go into town to have an extra meal! After a few days, we took the boat to the USA to Seattle, and after a night took the train right down the west coast of America, stopping at San Francisco, where Hans met with a former pupil, and then on to Los Angeles. Some friends that we knew drove us for the day into Mexico, where they had a farm which grew cashew nuts. Unlike the USA, which we had just visited, Mexico was very crowded and full of people. From this place we flew home to London. It was a most interesting journey that I shall never forget.

In April 1991, we flew to St Lucia to stay with my dear friend Dink and a colleague from my days at Teachers' College. She had married a handsome, tall West Indian man who had become a judge in the service of the British Empire. On his retirement, he was knighted, and Dink, believe it or not, was then called Lady Gordon. They lived by a beautiful harbour and in the early morning you could see the cruise boats gliding into the port. It was a very different place from anything that I had ever seen before. At Dink's insistence, we stayed on longer than we had originally intended. Therefore, we only spent one or two nights in Barbados. But it was good to stay longer with Dink and her husband.

We enjoyed many holidays during our retirement, but the ones I mentioned are the ones that stand out as being special. I will always remember Barbados, with its great mahogany trees.

When Hans retired, we had the leisure time to go on holidays. We went three times to South Africa, in 1976, 1989 and 1994. On these occasions we visited Pretoria to see my old friends Sarah and Norman Zway and the Hirschs in Johannesburg. On one occasion we hired a car and travelled through the Karoo to Cape Town.

In 1994, on the last occasion Erica went with us, the new elections, voting in the ANC, had not yet taken place, but Nelson Mandela (released from prison in 1990) was about to become the first African President.

We hired a car and drove inland to the wine-growing area of the Cape, where we stayed with my friend and former colleague Philippa Barry. We stayed in their picturesque farmhouse on their grape farm, with the mountains in the distance. We drove along the Garden Route, staying a few nights in Hermanus, where Erica met her old school friend Priscilla Thomas, and they swam in the sea. On our return, we stayed in a self-catering cottage set in the lush valley between Constantia Bay and Twelve Apostles Mountain.

On one occasion, I visited the former nursery school training centre that I had started. It was now part of a thriving and much-extended technical college. Many of my old pupils came to meet me. It was a happy occasion for all. For three days we stayed in a mountain chalet called Houtkapper's Poort.

While David was lecturing in America, the family all enjoyed staying in his Lewes house. Hans and I and the rest of the family (three grandchildren, Louisa, Esther and Jeremiah) enjoyed every aspect of our several summer holidays together. We would pack up a picnic basket and whenever the sun shone there we were on the beach at Seaford. Many happy hours were spent swimming in the sea, resting in Friston Forest and visiting Drusillas Zoo. The early-morning market in Lewes was a great delight, and we would come home laden with home-made cakes, flowers, knitted toys and fresh vegetables.

Chapter Thirty-Five.

CONSIDERING SOME CHANGES OVER THE YEARS

When I look back over my long life, I realise how much has changed in the way people live their lives today. In the past, information about current affairs was given only through the newspapers. There was no radio (wireless), no television, and, of course, no computers. We had telephones and would speak to the operator, usually a woman, who would ask 'Number, please?' when we picked up the phone to make a call. I remember certain numbers to this day. At Norwood we were Streatham 1676. My mother's number was Museum 2503.

Central heating did not exist in England. I remember when Hans and I came on a visit to London, a cousin of Hans called Ernie Ruben had installed central heating. Hans and I both thought it very unhealthy. As a child I had a coal fire in my bedroom. My aunt and uncle had a gas fire which they lit with a match, and it went pop. The advantage of a gas fire was that it could be turned on and off very easily.

The coal fire in my bedroom would go on glowing through the night. The light from the fire cast reflections on the ceiling. The fire was built up with scrunched-up newspaper, wood and coal. It was quite a knack to build a good fire, and sometimes where the coal did not

Chapter Thirty-Five. Considering some changes over the years

catch easily you could hold an open newspaper in front of the fire to create a draught in the chimney. But one had to be careful that the newspaper didn't catch fire! We had a tall fender around it for safety. Various items of washing would be hung along the fender, as there was no such thing as a tumble dryer or a washing machine. After the Second World War, in South Africa we bought a little Hoover washing machine. The clothes whirled around and afterwards we put them through a mangle, which had to be turned by hand.

People tended to sit close to the fire for warmth. We needed to wear more clothes than one does today. I remember as a little girl wearing socks and little boots which were done up with a button hook. We wore layers of underclothes, including a woollen vest, what is called a liberty bodice, which was made of very thick cotton.

My mother and aunts wore corsets made with whale-bones. They wdere laced at the back and hooked at the front. The whale-bones were moderately flexible. When I was about twenty years old, my mother said, 'You had better buy a corset or you will lose your figure.' I bought one of these whale-boned corsets and the assistant fitted me, pulling the lace tight at the back. I decided I would wear it on the way home. When I got on the bus, I dropped my fare of sixpence and couldn't bend down to pick it up! When I reached home, I took off the corset and never ever wore it again.

As I grew older, I wore woollen combinations. This was a vest with sleeves combined with some sort of loose knickers, similar to pantaloons. They were very warm and very ugly. My mother had bought the very thickest and best quality and I realised they would never wear out. By the time I was 15 or 16, I gave them up for more attractive underwear.

Women did not wear trousers. It was only some time later, perhaps when I was in my mid-thirties, before they became fashionable.

Instead, we wore winter skirts made of serge fabric and a blouse, cardigan or jersey on top. Clothes were not easily washed. Children wore a pinafore made of cotton, which covered them up and protected their clothes and was more easily washable.

In the summer, we wore cotton and silk dresses which had to be ironed. In the winter, we wore woollen stockings which were held up by garters or a suspender belt. As I grew very fast, I had a new winter coat every year, usually with a little fur or velvet collar. Hats were made of velour in the winter and straw in the summer. Straw hats were quite pretty. They could be decorated with a ribbon or imitation flowers. Ostrich feathers were fashionable. As I grew older, the liberty bodice was replaced with a sling bodice which was made by Kestos. It supported the breasts.

For parties or for best, one could have a velvet dress, or one made of taffeta or silk. Often, a pretty sash was wrapped around the waist. One wore gloves which were knitted or made of good leather. For extra warmth, a fur muff was hung by a cord around your neck, which would keep the hands even warmer in cold weather.

I do not think men's clothing has changed so much. Boys, of course, wore short trousers while they were young, and it was a great event when they went into 'longs'. Men's clothing was pretty conventional, and you rarely saw a man without a tie. Both boys and girls occasionally were dressed in sailor suits depicting the naval look.

Men often wore a waistcoat which matched their suits. The waistcoat had little pockets where they would keep a large watch and fob chain. If you asked them the time, they could take it out of their pocket. Hats were quite an important article of clothing. Working class people wore caps. Men in the city wore bowler hats, or they could choose a Trilby or a Homberg. Top hats could be worn on special occasions. In the summertime, the men wore straw hats.

Chapter Thirty-Five. Considering some changes over the years

Where did we buy our clothes? Clothes mattered a great deal to my mother and aunts. We usually attended the opening day of the winter sales. We especially went to the sale at Bourne & Hollingsworth in Oxford Street. My mother usually found a pretty party dress for me, much reduced in price. She would then go around all the departments looking for bargains. And the firm were quite prepared to send the purchases home for us.

Sales were not as busy as they are today, but they were quite an event. I remember my mother's bargain of the year from Whiteleys: a fur coat for five pounds. My mother was very adept at choosing clothes and knew what would suit and fit every member of the family. Had she lived in another age, she could easily have been a buyer for a department store, but this was in the 1920s. I can see my aunts trying on the various clothes, and if they didn't like them they would say, 'This will do for our Clara in Liverpool.'

We also went to a secondhand clothes shop in Store Street, quite near to Chenies Street. It was run by someone called Madame Isippi. She had remarkably beautiful dresses brought in by lady's maids. They were usually designer dresses, and they had only been worn once or twice. We found the clothes irresistible and, in fact, we called the shop a death trap. I think Madame Isippi was there until the beginning of the Second World War; but, of course, I was in South Africa by then.

Changes with regard to the food

As far as food was concerned, there was very little prepared in advance. Ready-made food was unusual. Both at Norwood and at my mother's hotel, food was prepared by a well-trained cook. The children at Norwood had very thick bread, which they called doorstops.

They had stews of various kinds prepared for the midday dinner and a roast for the Sabbath. The only food that came in prepared was fried fish from the East End. Enough for 450 children! And saveloys from Barnets, the kosher butcher. Chicken was a luxury in those days, much more than beef. At the weekend, the staff were treated to chicken soup, with the chicken served separately with vegetables. We did not have roast chicken.

There was no such thing as yoghurt, and ice cream was a luxury. Desserts were rice pudding, sago and tapioca. I didn't like the last two very much at all. There was also steamed pudding topped with treacle, which was delicious, as well as jam tarts. And there was a certain amount of fruit, too.

At Christmas-time, you could buy tangerines wrapped in silver paper and apples, bananas, pears and very occasionally a grapefruit or grapes. Pomegranates only came in the winter. It was great fun to buy a whole coconut, drain it off and drink the milk, and then break the coconut itself, probably with a hammer or an iron. Roasted chestnuts could be bought in the street daily.

Chapter Thirty-Six.

LOOKING BACK OVER THE YEARS

Looking back over my long life, I realise how many good friends I have made. All my dear school friends have passed away. I remember my Aunt Esther, who died a few days short of the age of 104. My mother was staying with me in Dunstan Road when, at the age of eighty-nine, she fell and broke her hip. The operation to mend it was successful, but sadly, after another two days, she died in the hospital. My cousin Marcus passed away at the age of eighty-five. He went into intensive care and Erica and myself were with him when he died. David returned from the USA.

My dear husband, after 69 years of marriage, passed away in 2007 at the age of ninety-eight, and I have had to adapt myself to a very different life. Towards the end of his life he had the early signs of dementia, but this did not alter his character. His talent for singing and his remarkable bass voice was as strong as ever. All his activities – giving concerts, singing in shul choirs and entertaining old people in the Old Age Homes – came to an end, although he was still able to entertain family and friends at home with the songs which we all loved. He is often in my thoughts and his presence is still with us.

I have also lost my dear and only grandson Jeremiah under tragic and unexplained circumstances. We are still investigating what happened when he went to Germany, mistakenly thinking he could join a protest conference against the Iraq War, but it turned out to be something much more sinister.

Reflections

I am fortunate in being so well cared for by my daughter Erica, who now lives with me, my son David and by my many carers. David lives on the Sussex coast and is in close touch every day and makes frequent visits to see me. I have three Granddaughters: Erica's daughters Louisa and Esther. David's daughter Leah. Louisa is a professional musician and plays the harp with many orchestras all over the country, as well as other parts of the world, and this year is even working in Japan. From when Louisa was a little girl, the two of us enjoyed singing together while I played the piano. Esther is now an experienced social worker dealing with many complex cases in London and Hertfordshire. Leah is about to start studying for A-levels at Brighton and Hove Sixth Form College, after achieving very successful grades at the Priory School in Lewes.

After I joined the B'nai B'rith Leo Baeck Lodge, I made many good friends. Over the years, there would be too many to mention.

And so the years went by. My mother, my aunts and uncles passed away, as well as most of my cousins, and many of my good friends.

I have lived now for sixty years in Dunstan Road, Golders Green. This is longer than I have lived anywhere else. Often, people ask me: to what do you attribute your long life? My first response would be: frankly, I really don't know; but on second thoughts I will answer that it is partly genetic and also because I do regular physical exercises every morning, had a good husband, enjoyed many interests that kept me occupied, as well as having the support and company of good friends.

Chapter Thirty-Six. Looking back over the years

I am now partially sighted and hard of hearing.

Erica married in 1973 and she had a home in Corringham Road, which was not far from us. Here, her children were born: Louisa in 1975, Esther two years later and Jeremiah in 1980. Living so near to us, Hans and I enjoyed being with them as they grew up.

David, who was born during the Second World War in 1942, lived in many places before he was eight: in Kimberley, Potchefstroom and Cape Town. He studied visual arts at Cape Town University. He re-married in 2002 and has a lovely daughter named Leah Charlotte, who is now sixteen years of age.

I have one dear cousin, Ruth, who is nine and a half years younger than me, who lives outside Belfast in Ireland. We speak on the phone to one another and I keep in touch with her and her two daughters, Noelle and Sally. I am still in contact with Hans's cousin's daughter Miriam, who lives not far away in Golders Green. She is part of the Charedi community.

Although I have lost so many of my friends and family, I have still been fortunate enough to make new friends.

I have several carers who come in daily to help me. They are interesting people and come from different parts of the world: two from Ireland, one from the Philippines, as well as Jamaica, Madeira and Eritrea. This makes it possible for me to remain in my own home, which gives me much pleasure. The Association of Jewish Refugees (AJR) have, over the years, helped Hans and me whenever there was a need. They arranged for me to have a regular visitor called Amina Brightwell. We have become close friends and I always enjoy her visits.

At the time of writing, I am keeping well, although my hearing and eyesight are not as good as they were. I am unable now to read, but enjoy listening to CDs which come from the local Barnet Mobile Library, RNIB (Royal National Institute of Blind People) and Jewish Care. When I am alone, I recall the many songs and poems and enjoy turning them into tonic sol-fah. I can remember things I learnt when I was only two or three years old. I think if I wrote them down, it would fill volumes. I still enjoy walking round my garden and sitting on the veranda in the sun. I also like to play the piano, although I can no longer see well enough to read music or see the keys.

Three years ago, I started to attend a class which encouraged us to write our life stories. The class was tutored by a very empathetic teacher, Helen Harris. A group of us still meet regularly to share our work in progress.

I will end this memoir with a description of my hundred and fourth-birthday party that Erica arranged. Forty-five guests enjoyed a special tea party at Stephen's House. The building originally belonged to Stephen's Ink, who was the founder of this famous product. It was a fine day and my forty-five guests arrived for the celebration a half an hour before tea was to be served. Guests were able to see the short film of our wedding taken in 1939, which was one of the first home movies to be shot in colour in South Africa. My family put up a collection of interesting photographs, beginning with my picture as a baby. Friends were seated at six tables and a truly delicious tea was served. Each table had a programme, and on the front was a picture of me dressed as a fairy. The tables were given the name of a place where I had lived during my life in England. These were Ferngrove, Liverpool, Knights Hill, West Norwood, Chenies Street, Westbourne Terrace, Inverness Terrace and now Dunstan Road.

After the tea, we had a most enjoyable concert by a Russian musician, named Igor, who sang a selection of Russian songs, accompanying himself on his accordion. Bernard Barnett sang, and we cut the chocolate birthday cake made by Diane. At the end I gave a speech about my life. As I cannot see to read the speech, I had to think it out carefully beforehand. I explained why each table was named, and that gave me the opportunity to describe the places where I had lived in England.

Rabbi Harry Jacobi spoke, and finally Rabbi Mark Goldsmith ended with the reading of Psalm 104. It was a very special occasion, and I was surrounded by good friends and my loving family. The happy memory of that party will stay with me forever.

I am now 106 years old, and this year I had a series of smaller parties to celebrate a long and full life. I have received over the years four cards from the Queen – these were displayed alongside the many cards from my dear friends.

Why did I write this book? Partly to remind myself of past events and partly as a record for my family and friends. To end on a cheerful note, here is a quote from one of my favourite songs:

Goodbye old thing, Cheerio Chin Chin,

Nah-poo, toodle-oo,

Goodbye-eeeee ...

Son David with my grand-daughter Leah.

Alyth Gardens Soup and Schmooze club. From left to right: Rabbi Josh Levy, Lynette Sunderland, Lucille Cohen, Selina Gilbert

2019. Some of my Devoted Carers.

Maria with flowers from our garden.

Catherine and I sit together.

Jocelyn and I walk around the garden.

Andrene and I look at my cards received from the Queen.

104th birthday party. Myself, with son David and grand-daughter Leah.

*2019. 107TH Birthday.
My daughter Erica, myself and my grand-daughter Esther.*

2019. 107th Birthdays. Myself and my grand-daughter Louisa'

104th Birthday Party. From left Esther, Sally, Leah, David, myself, Erica, Noel, Alanna

At my 106th Birthday with cards received over time from the Queen.

www.ingramcontent.com/pod-product-compliance
Lightning Source LLC
Chambersburg PA
CBHW052017070526
44584CB00016B/1793